BABY GANESH COLORING BOOK

for kids & adults

+50 pages

FOR FUN

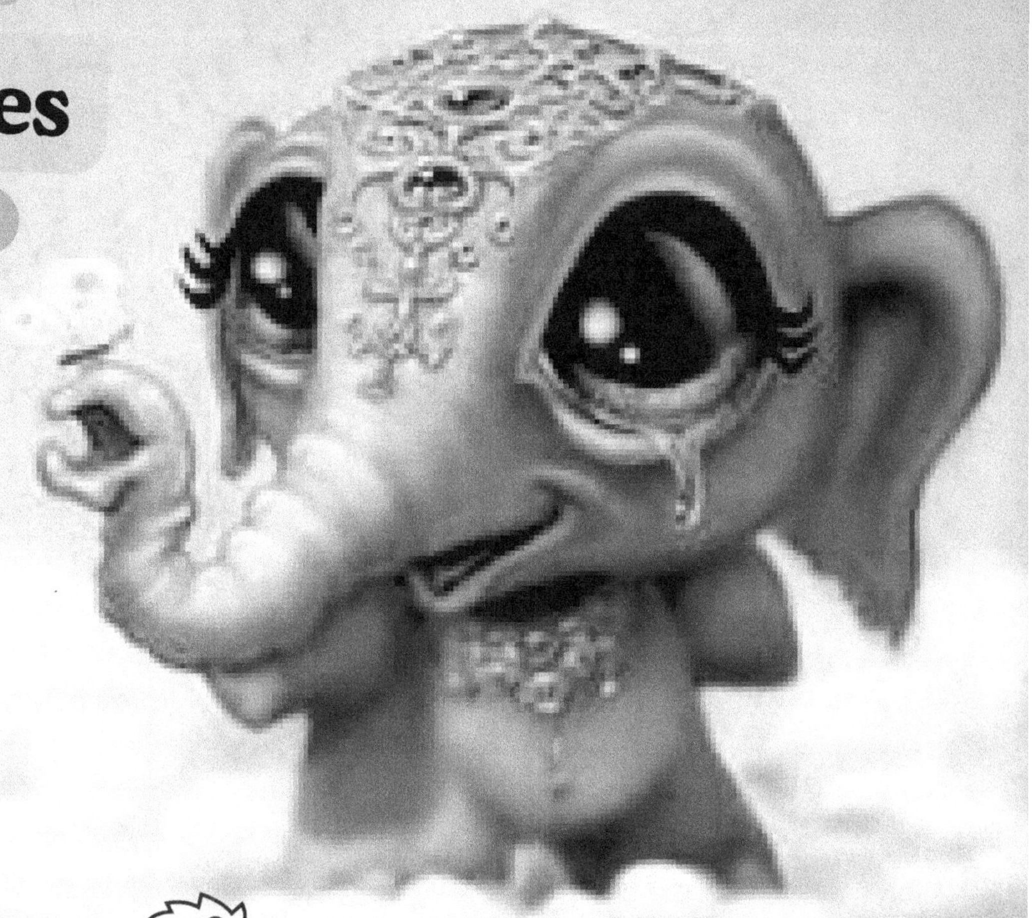

cacho
productos digitales

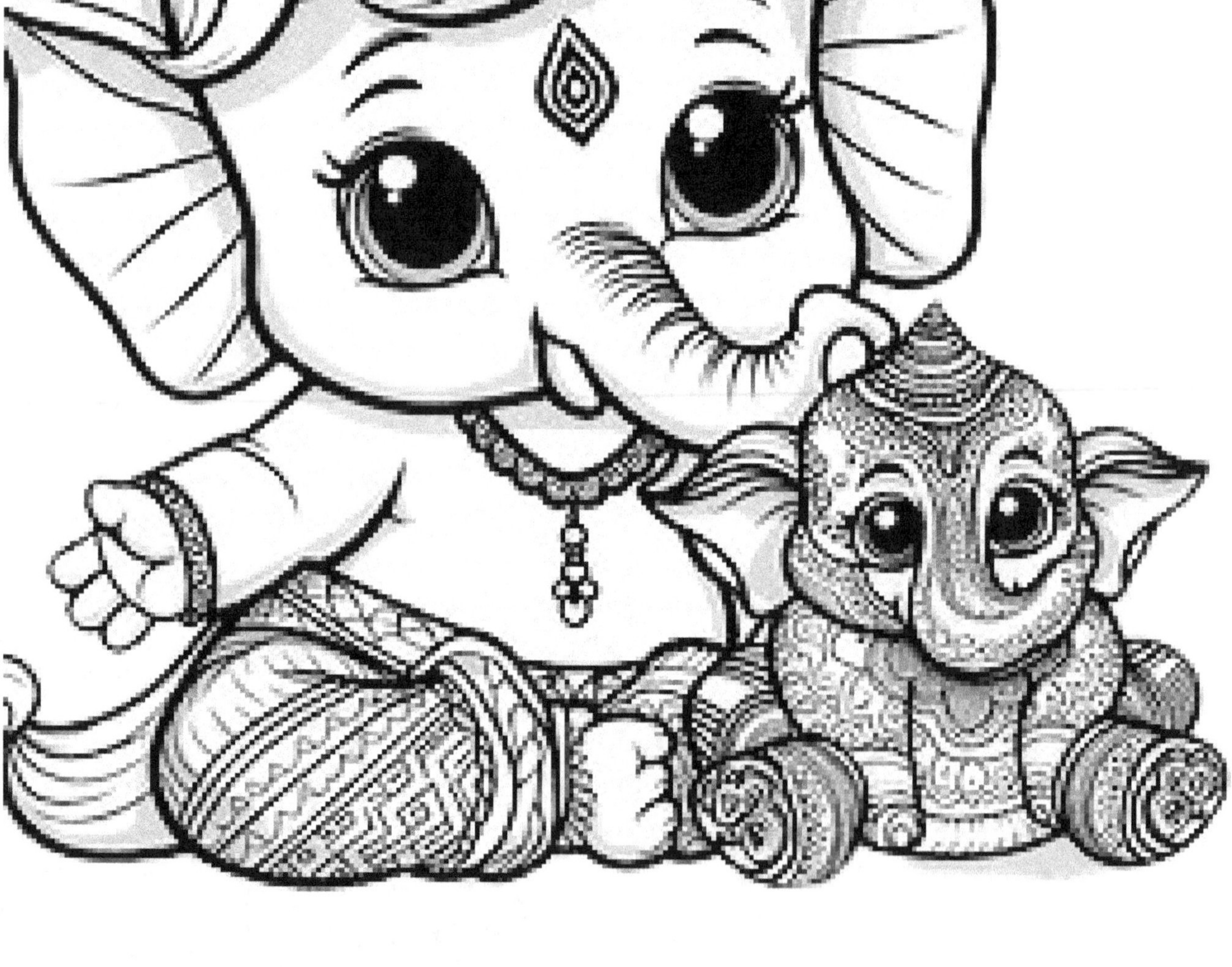

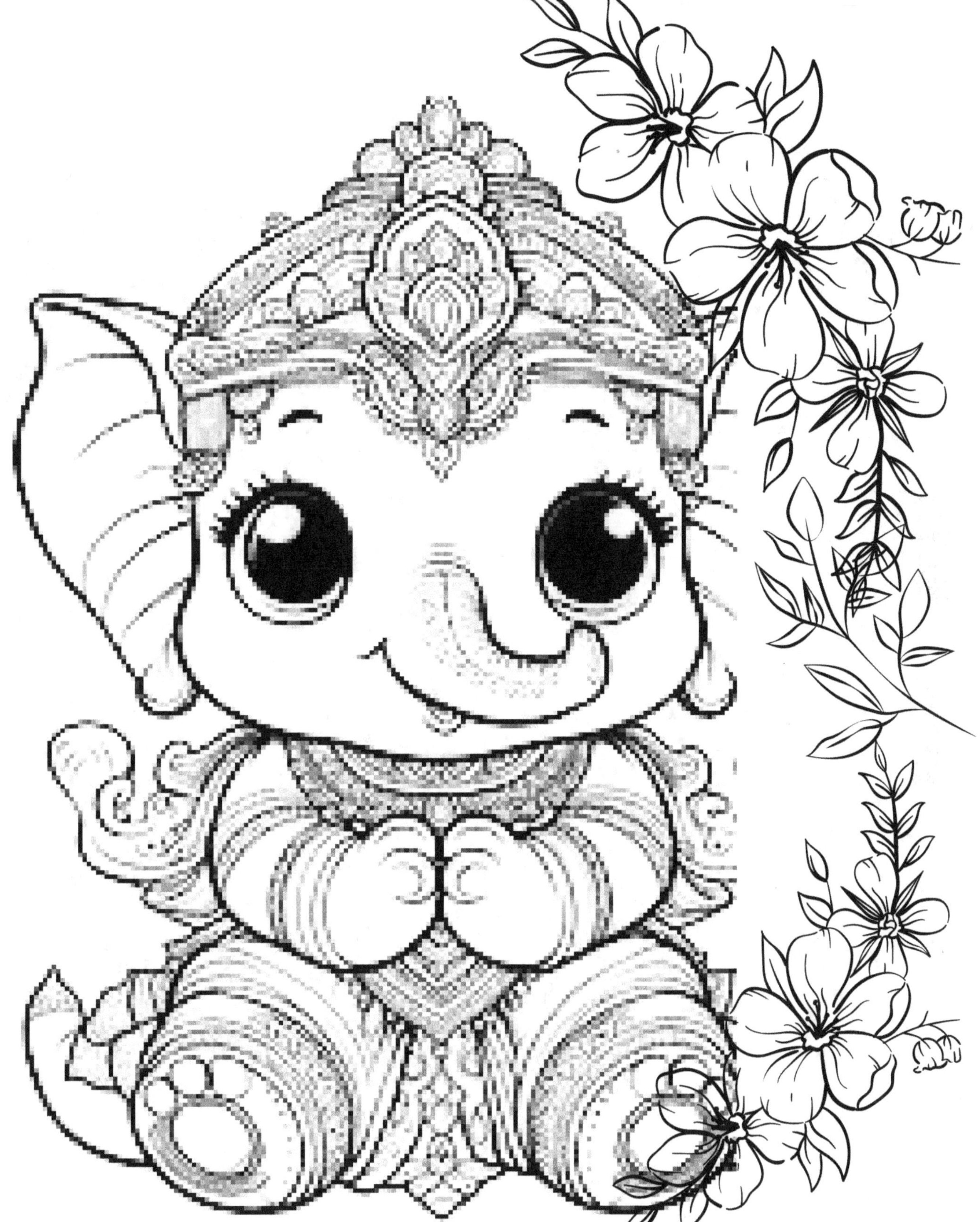

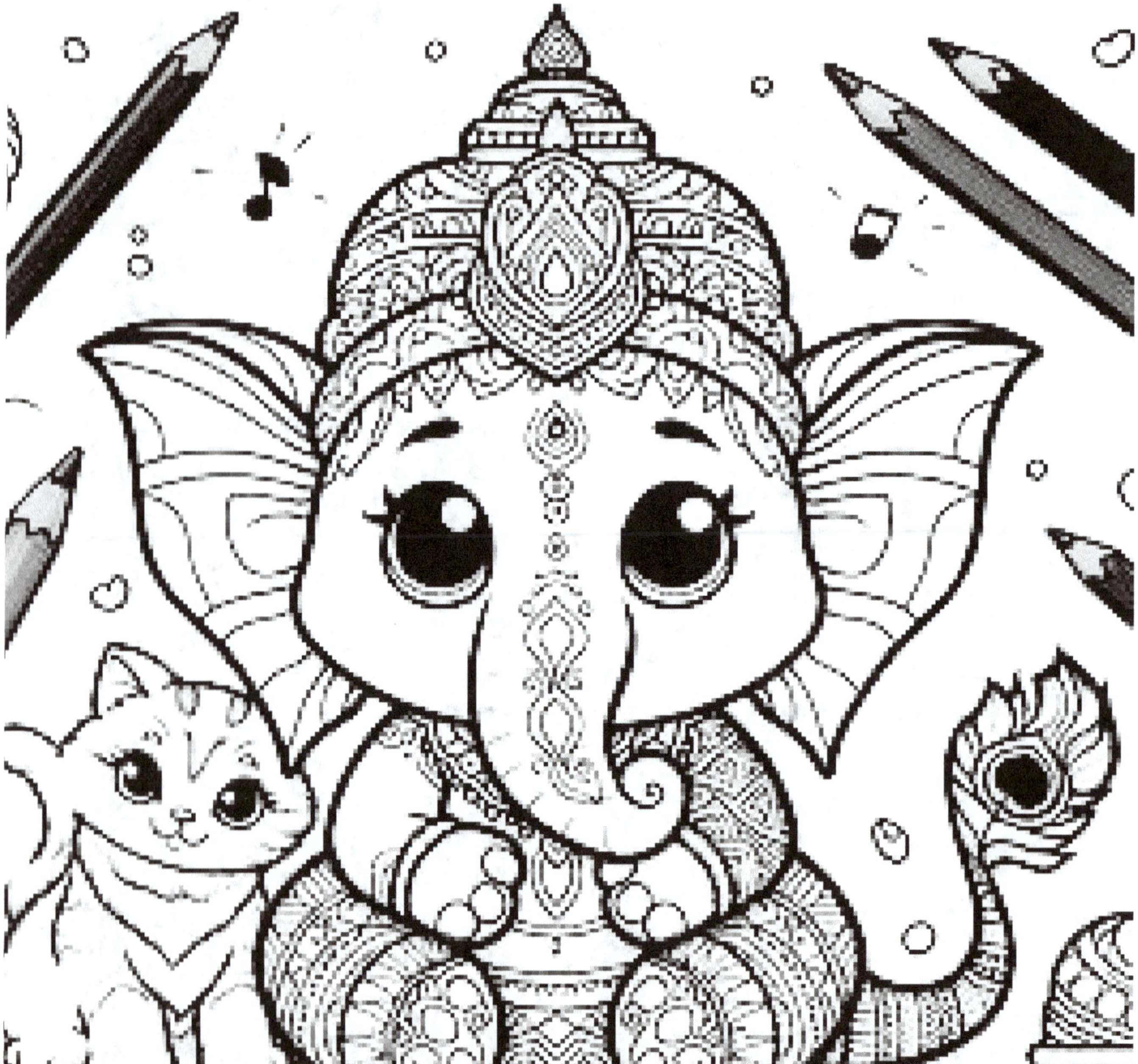

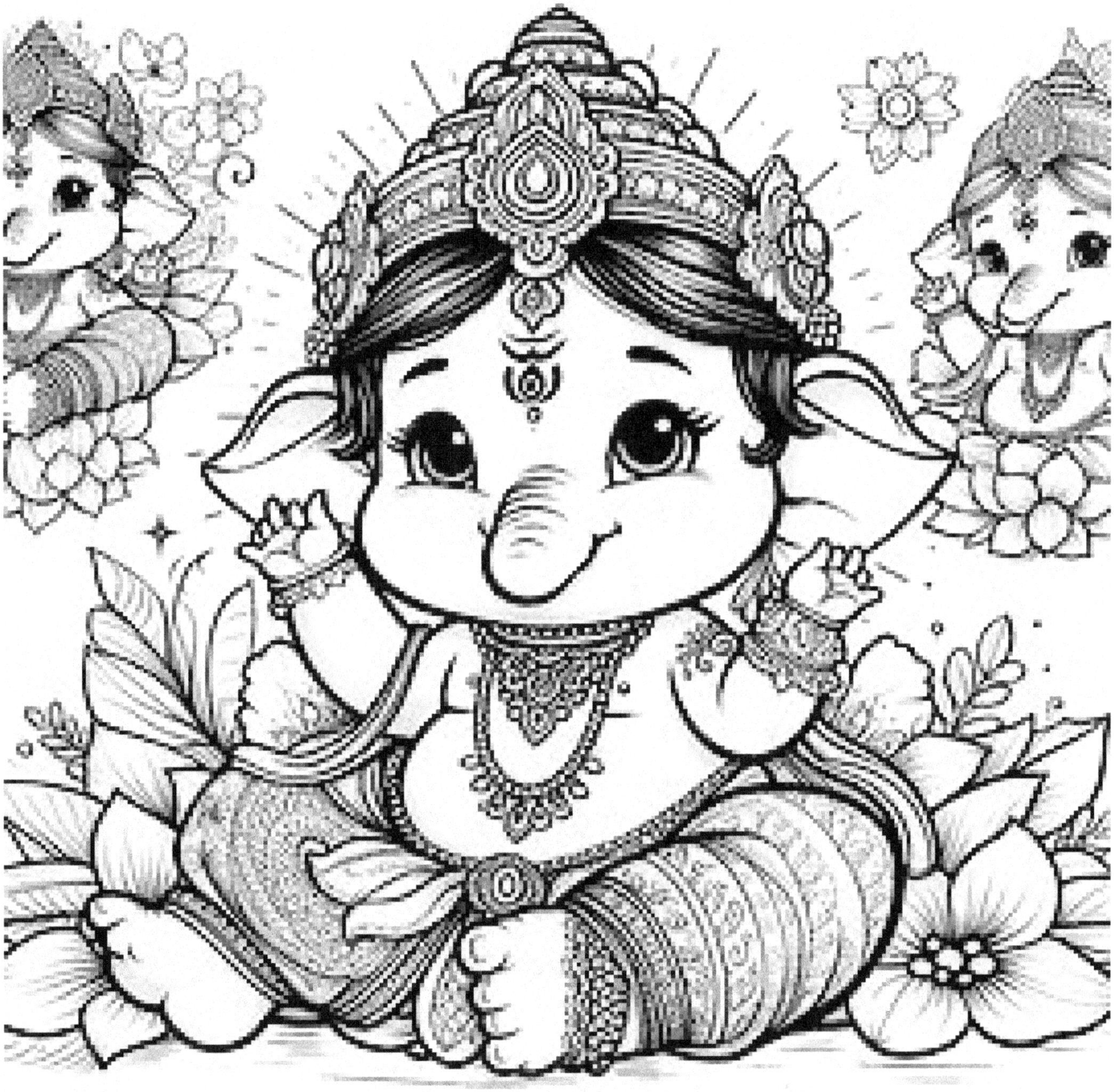

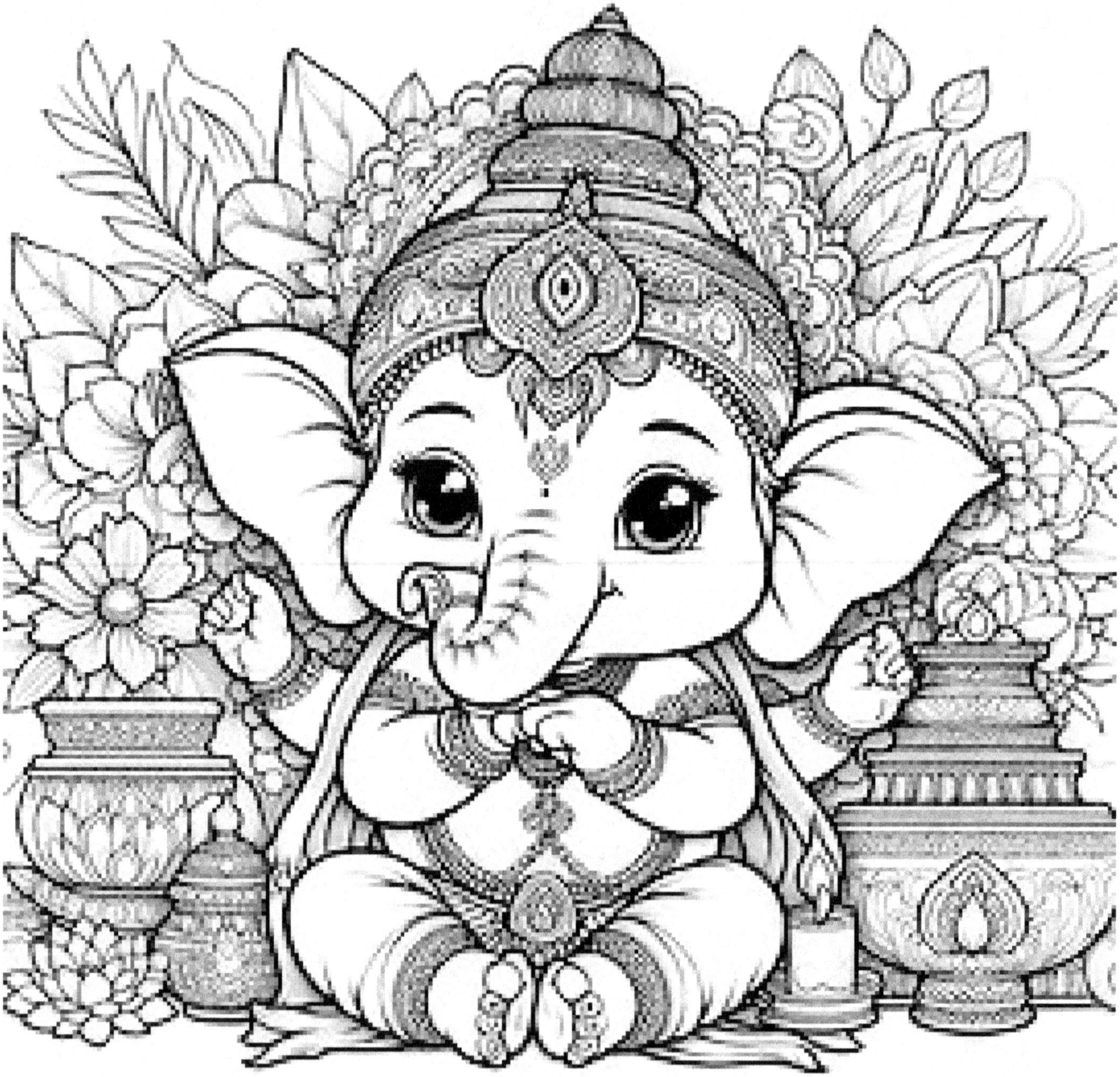

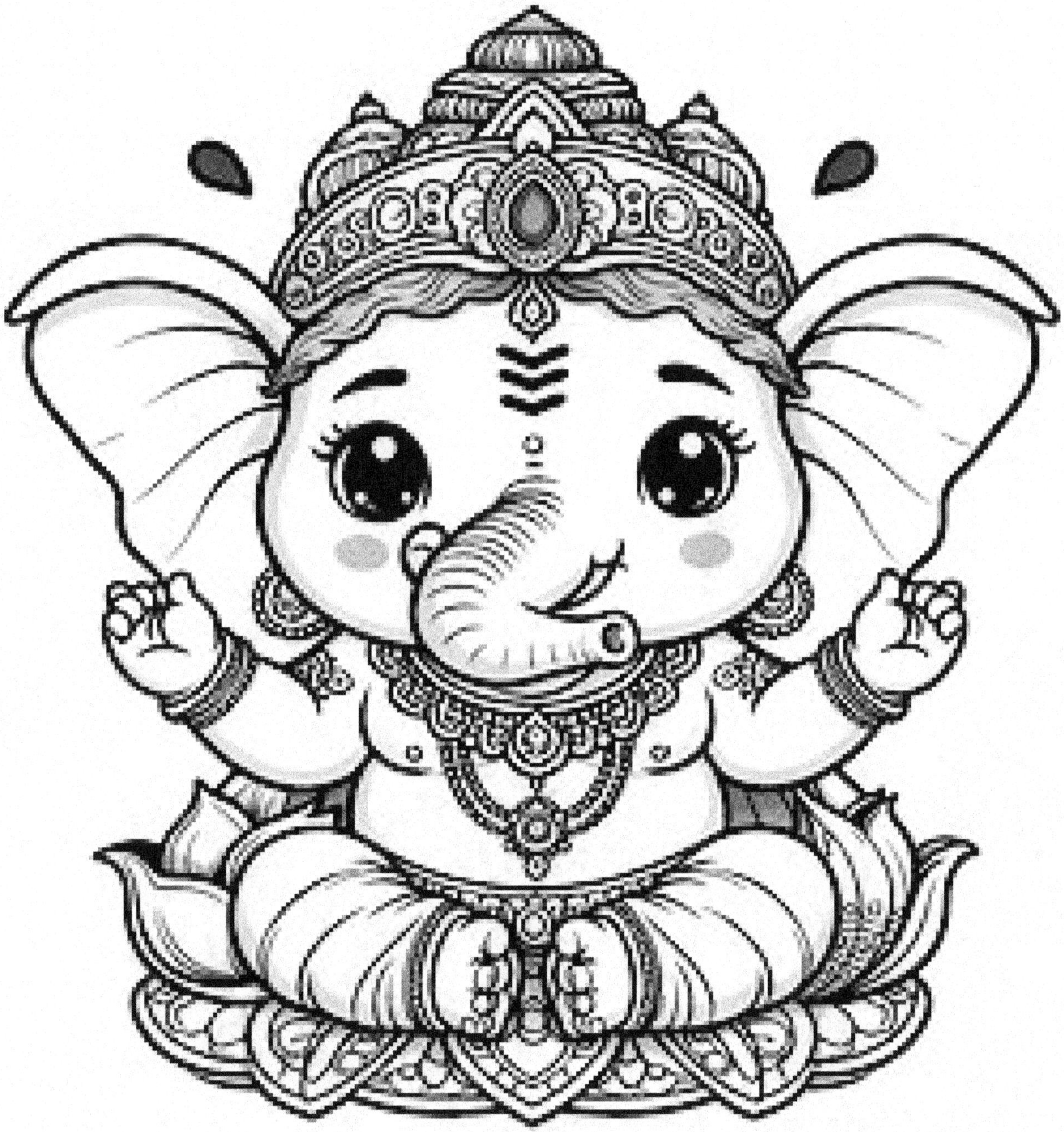

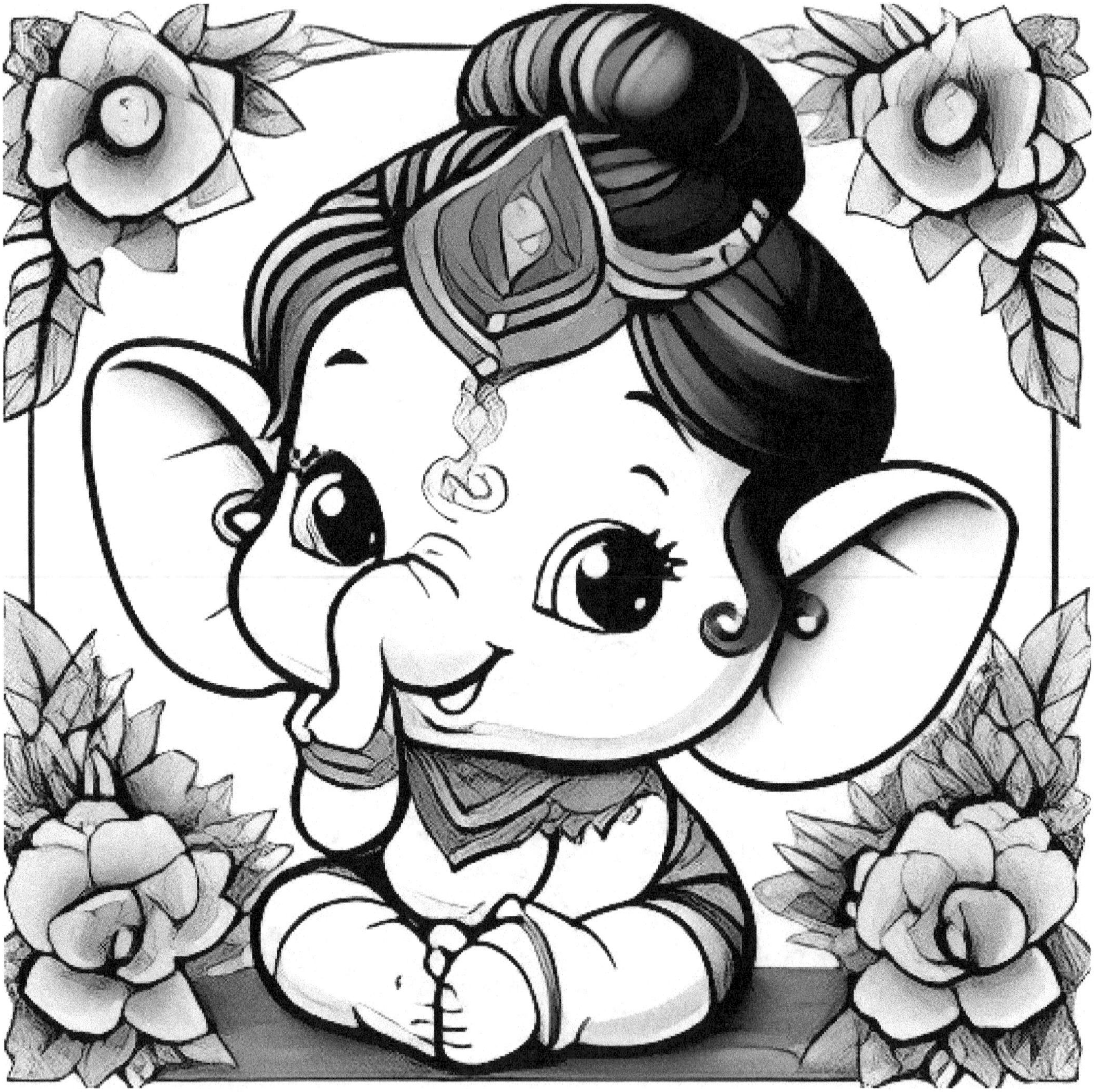

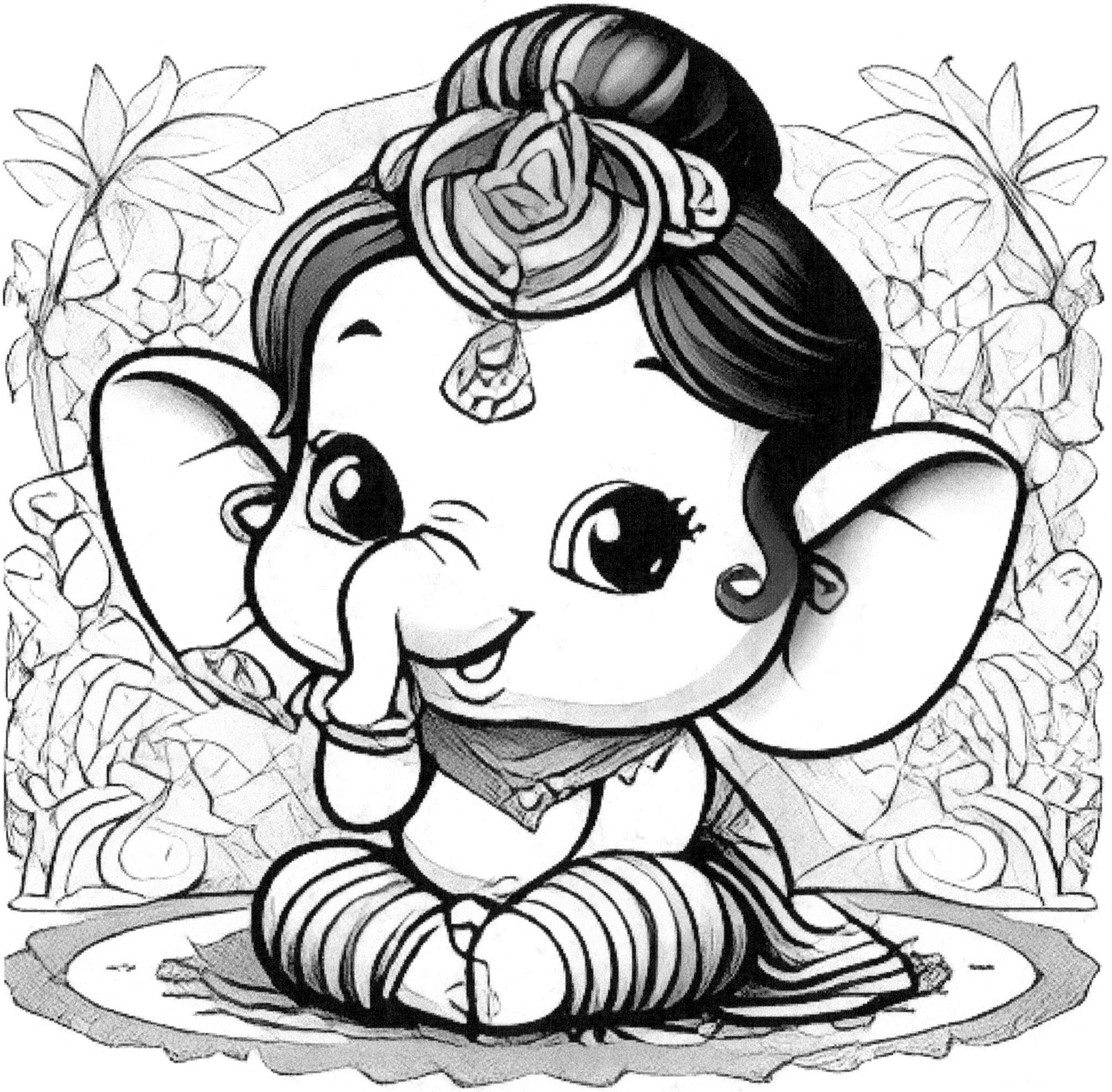

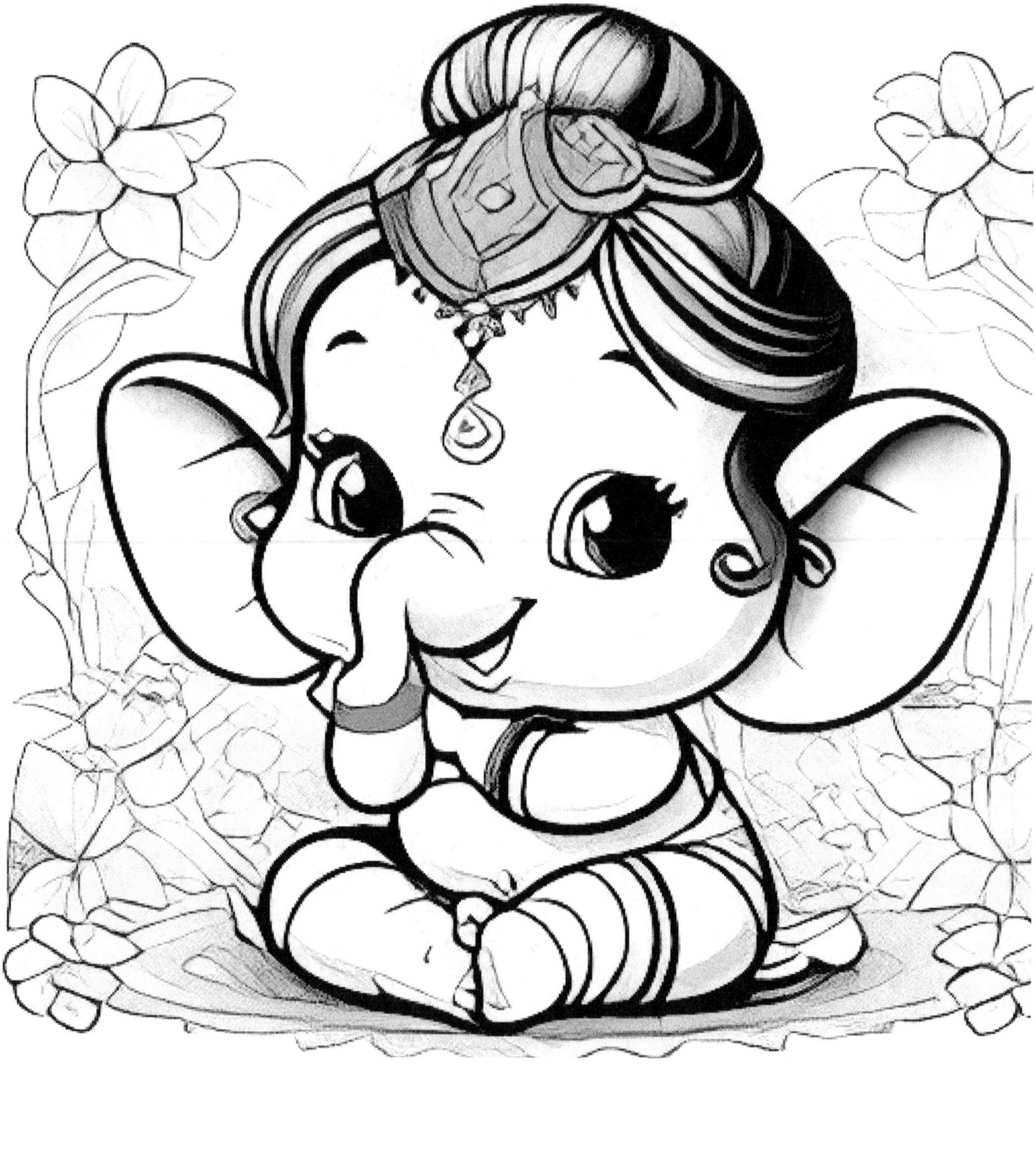

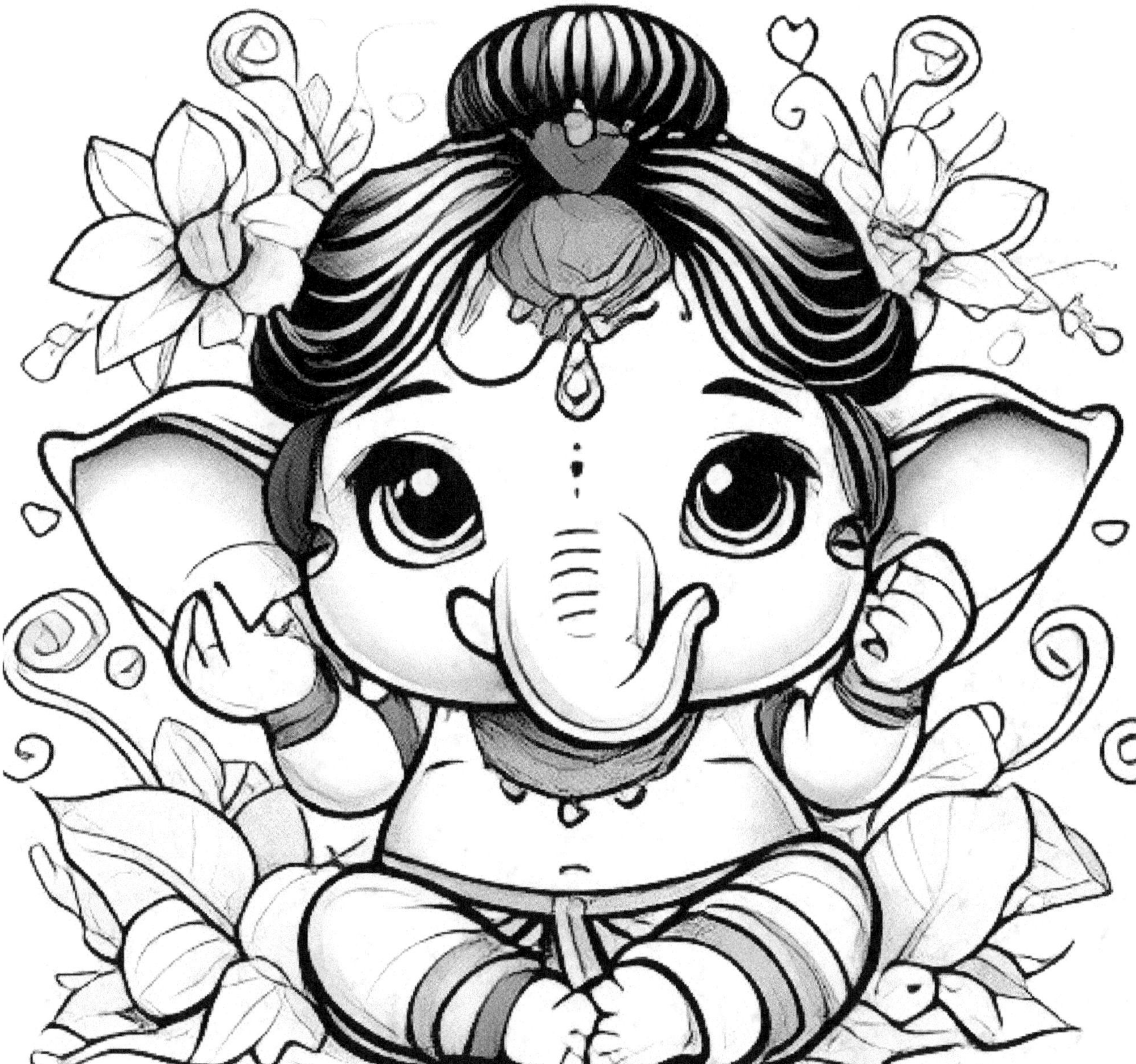

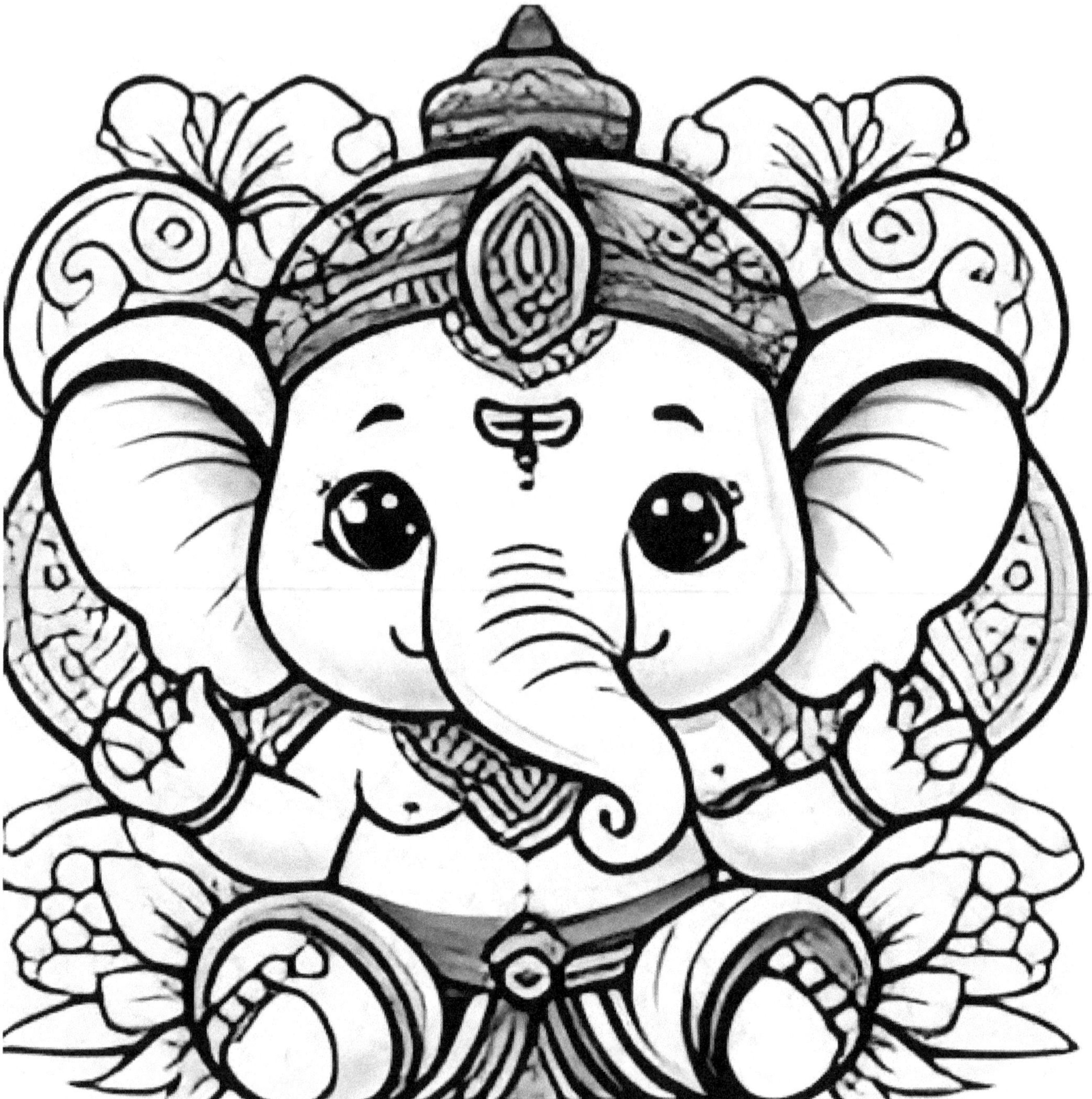

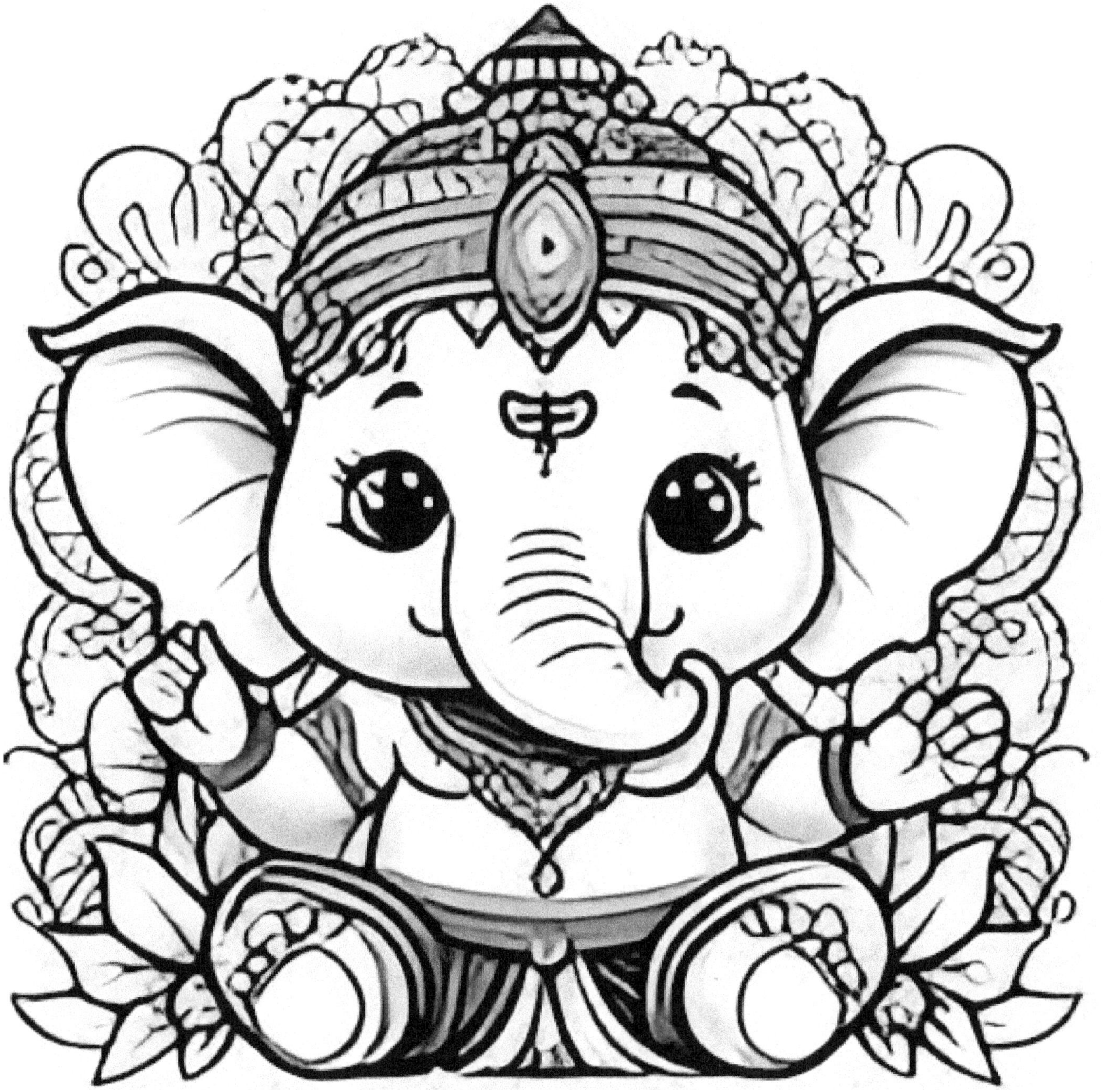

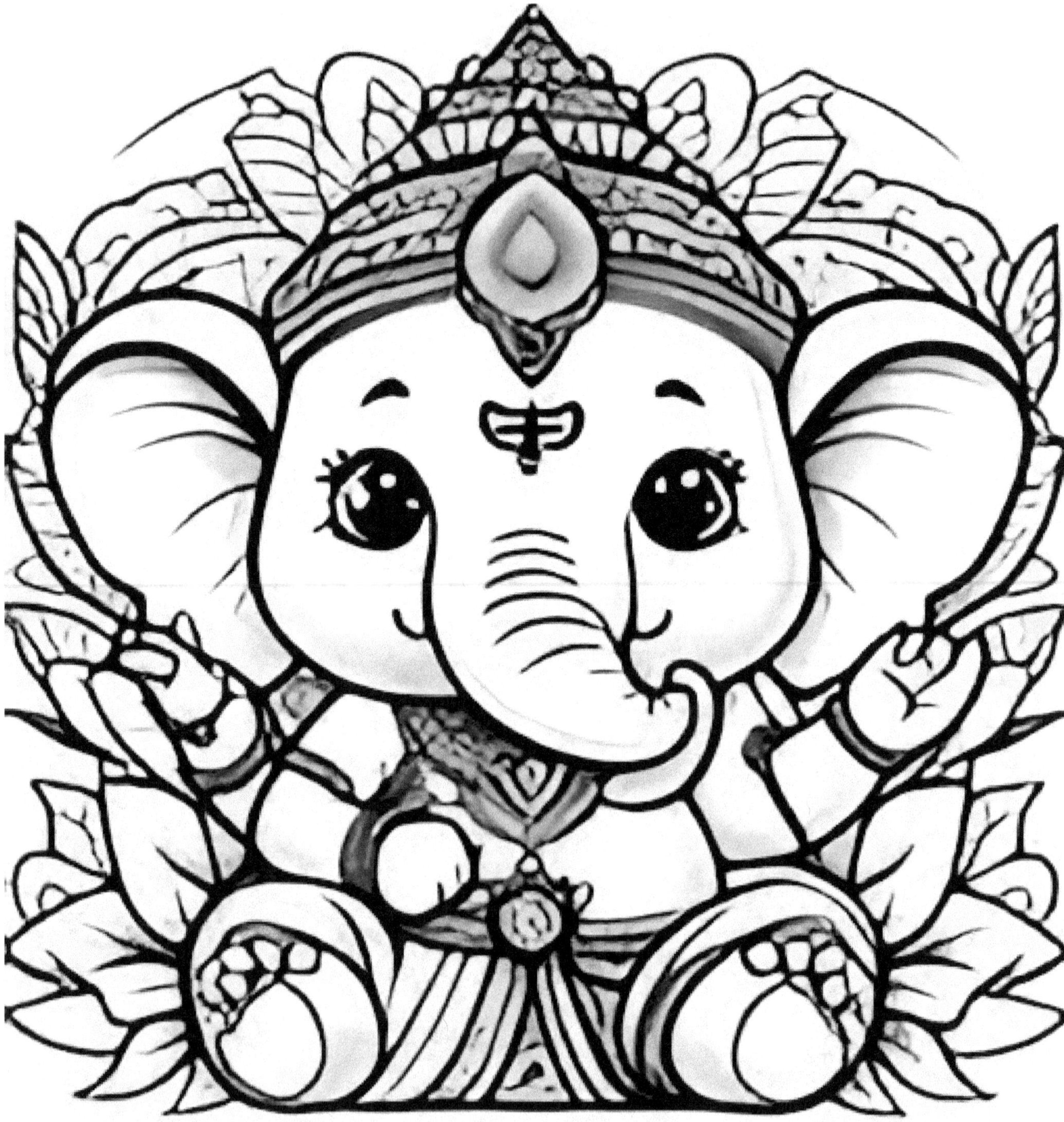

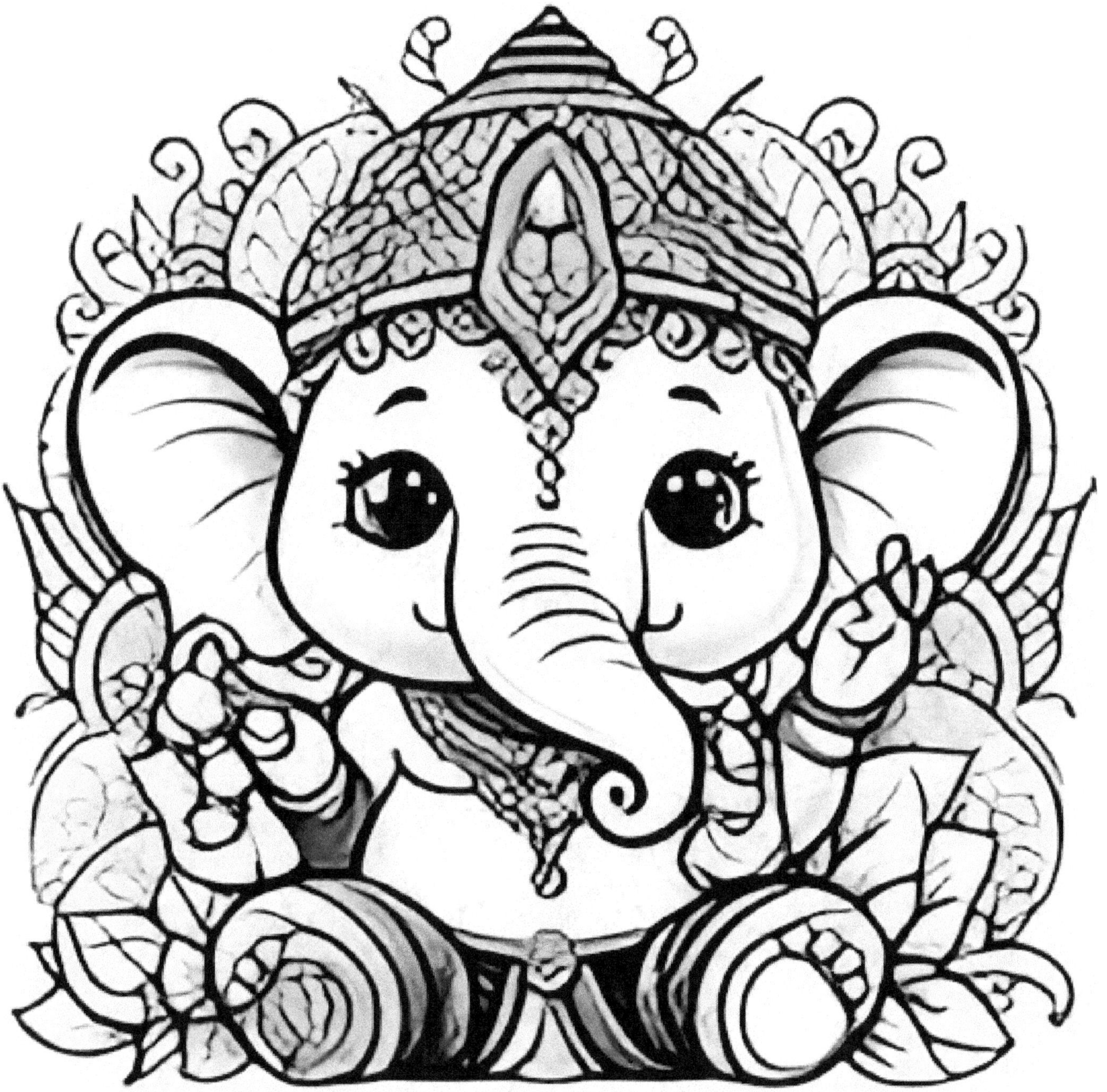

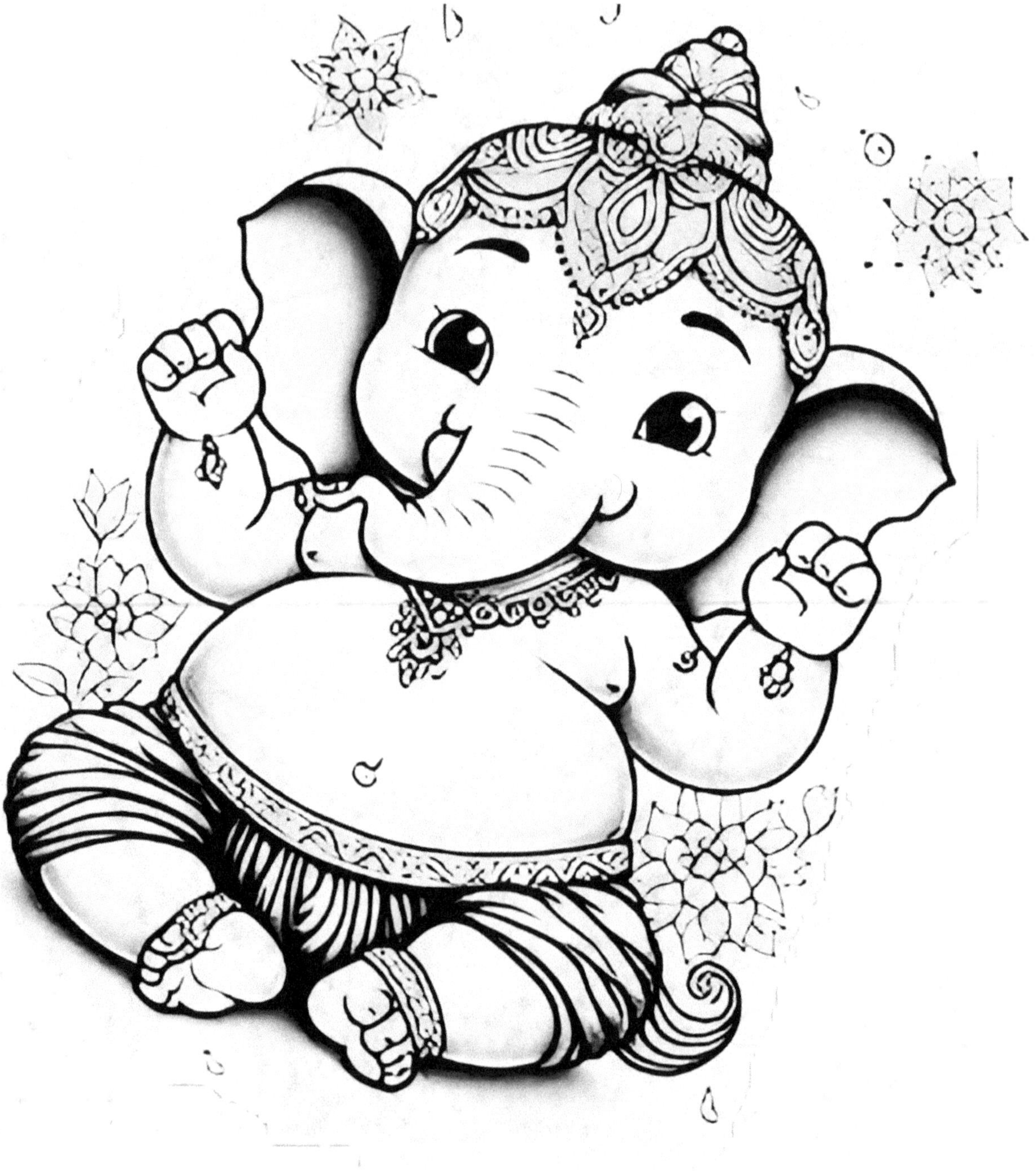

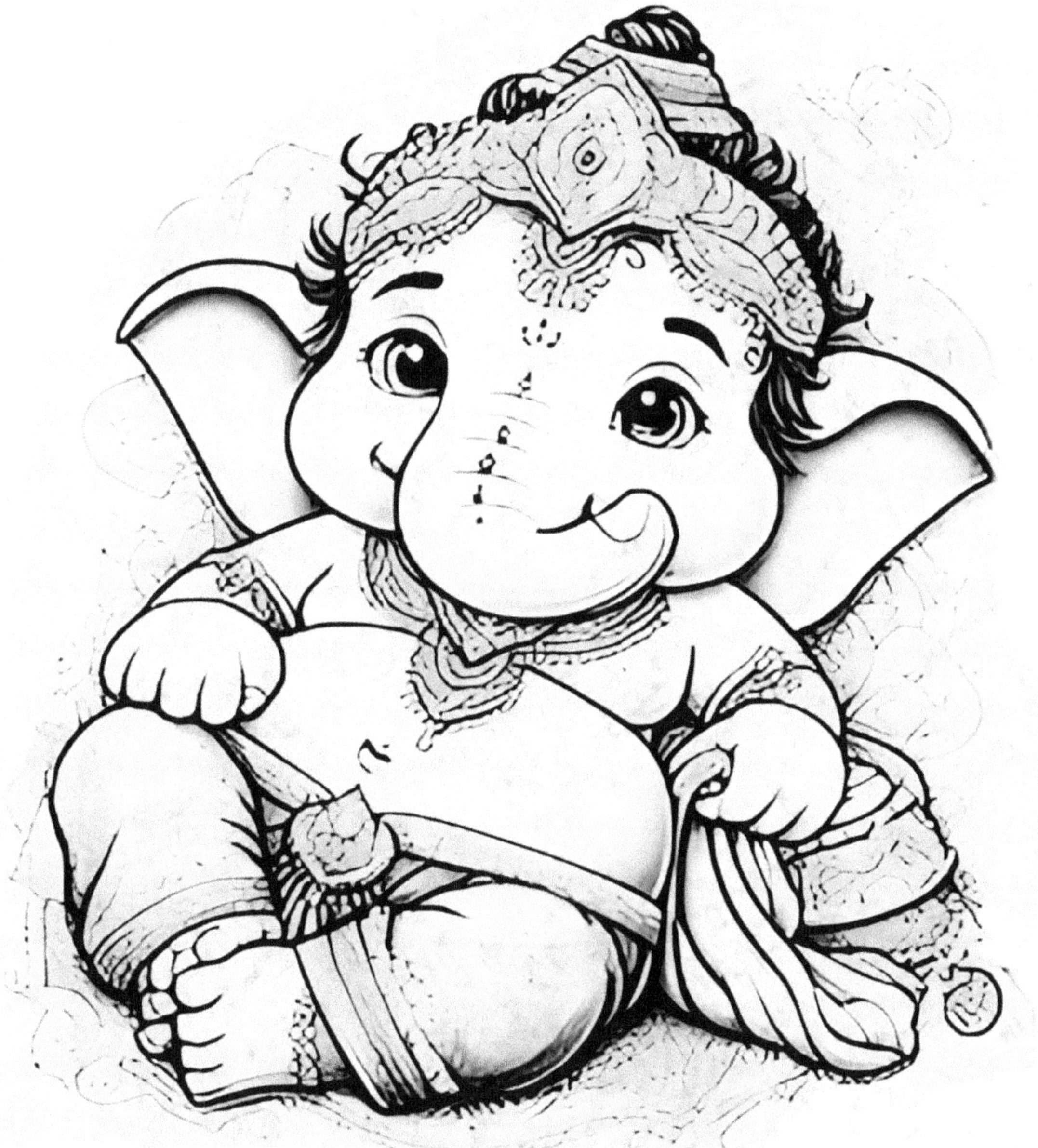

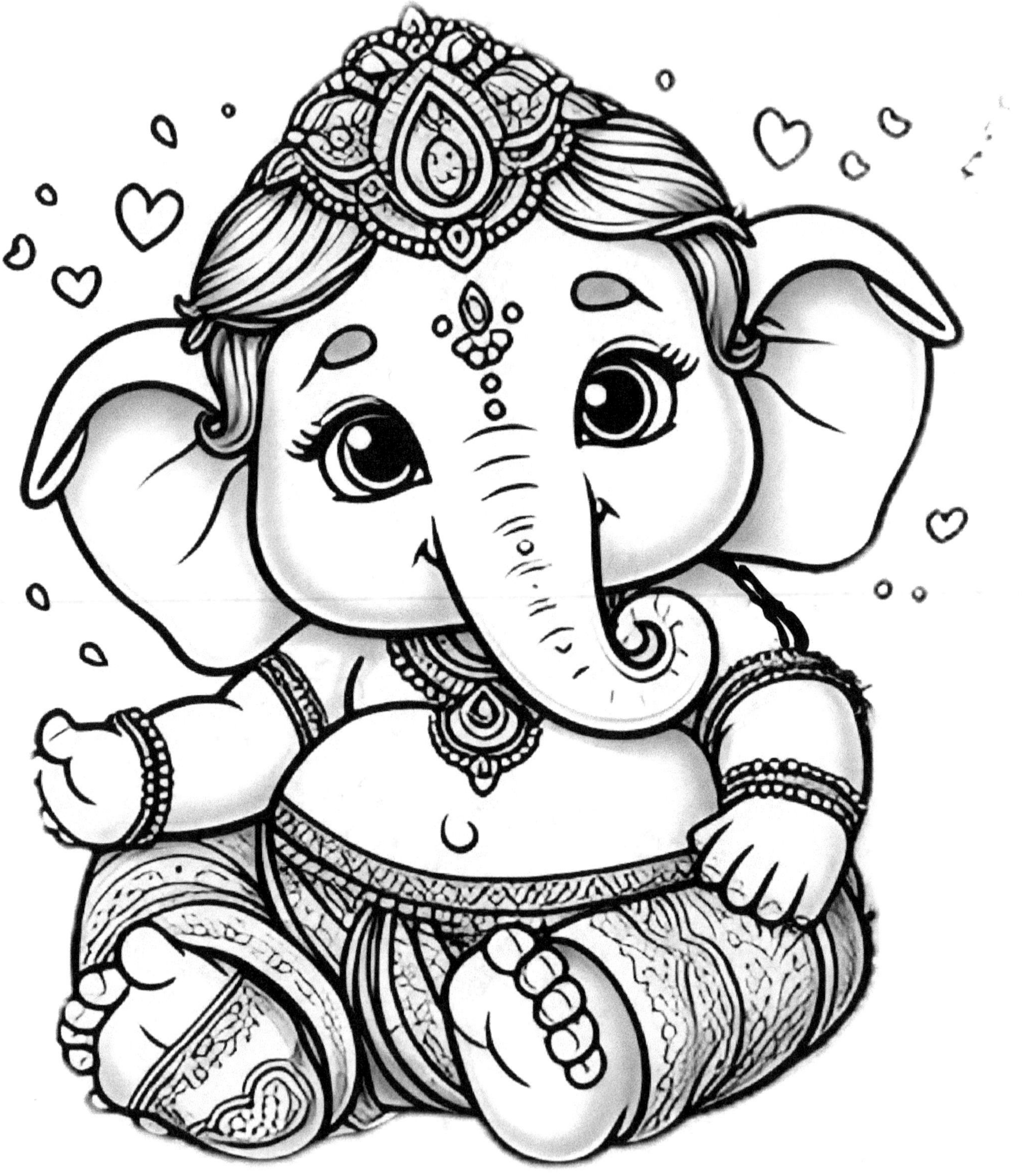

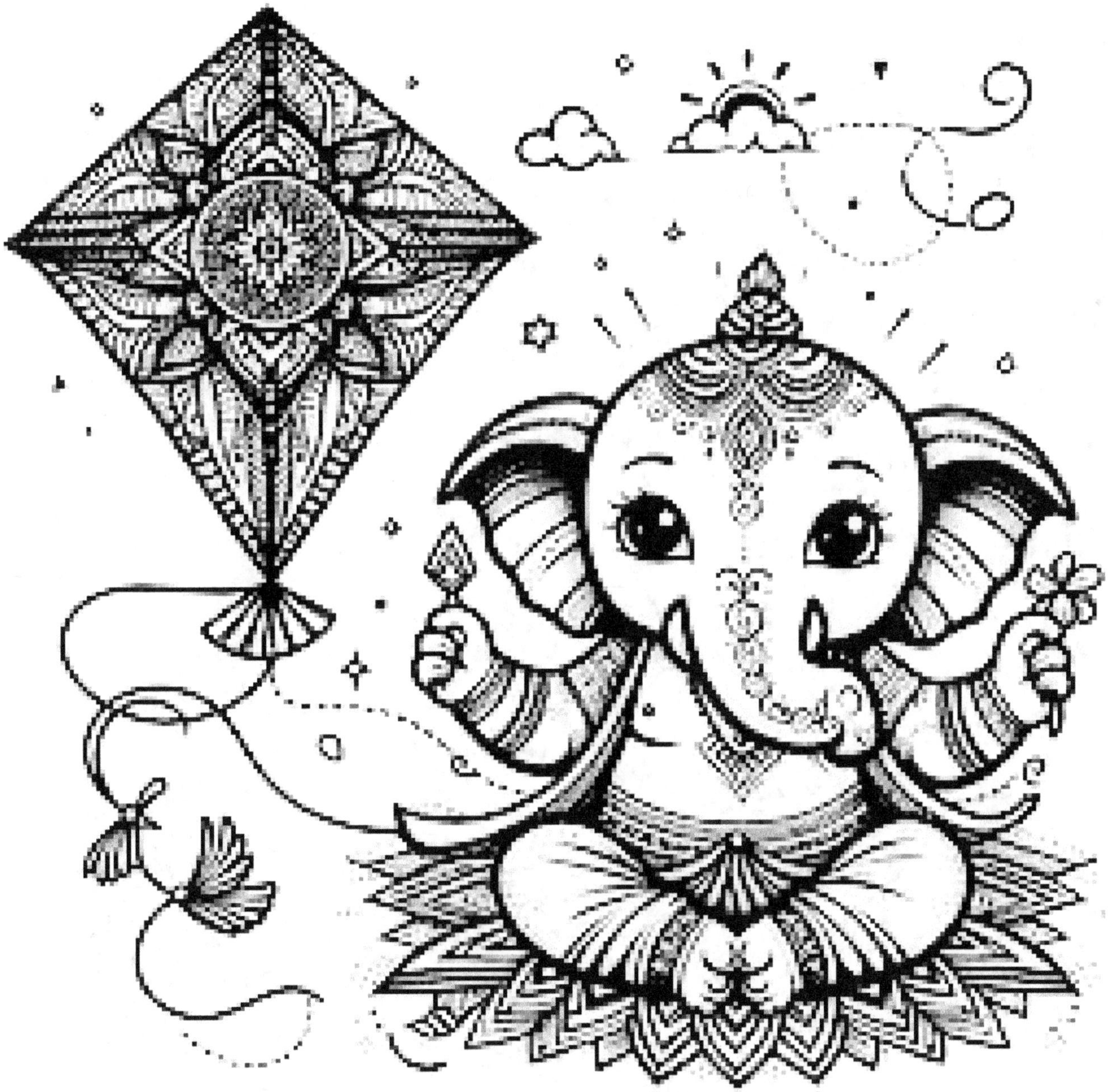

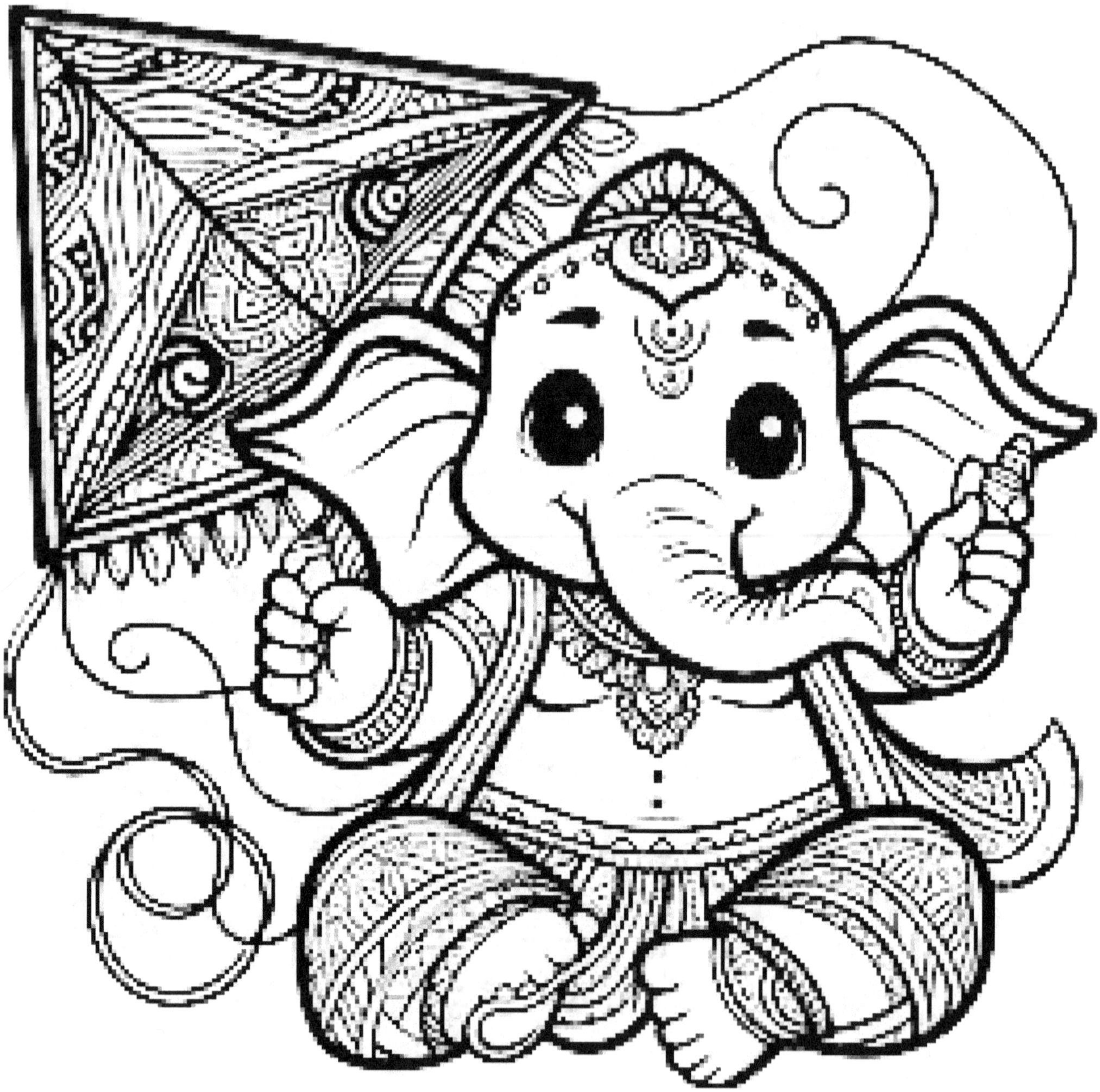

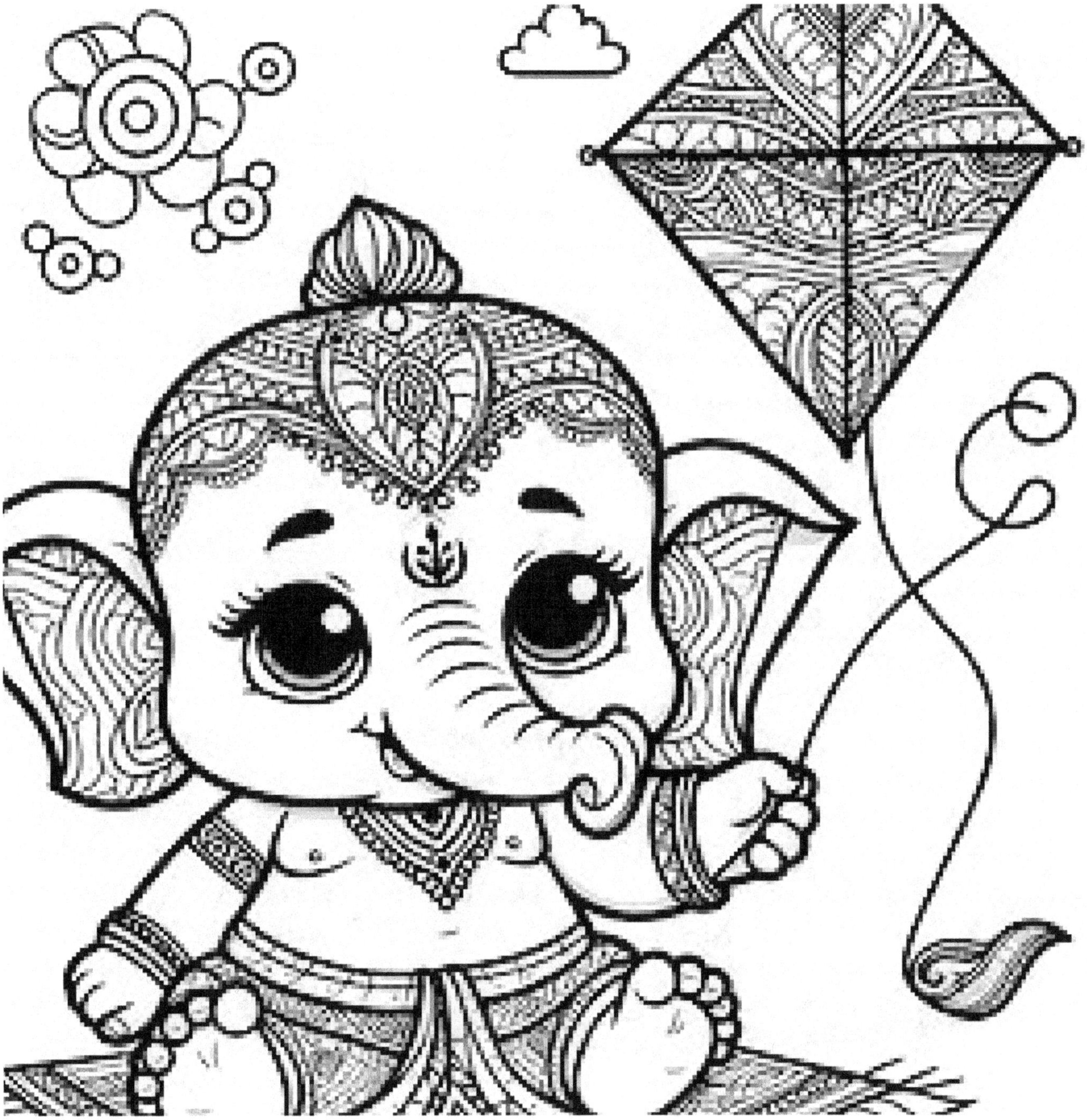

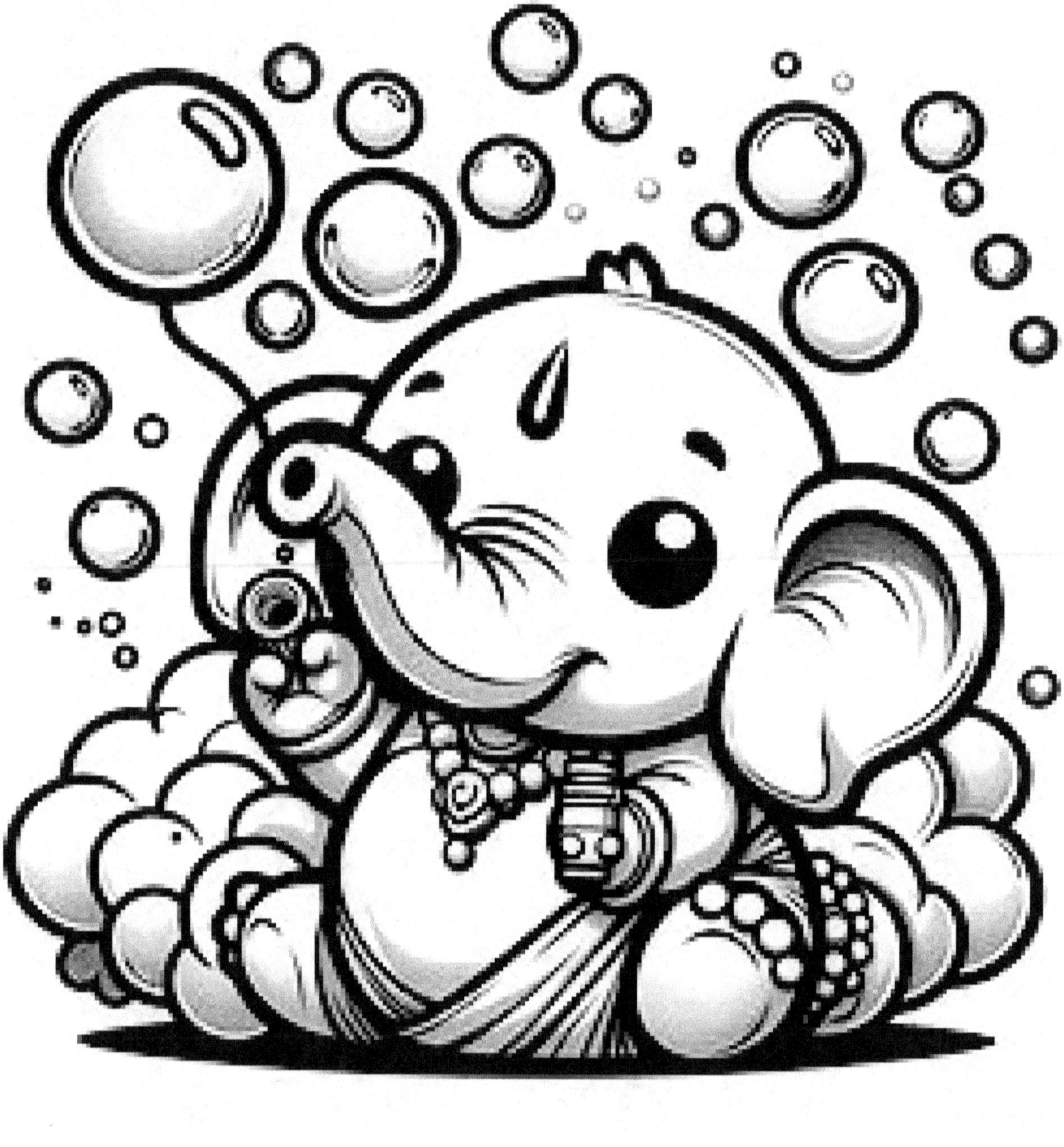

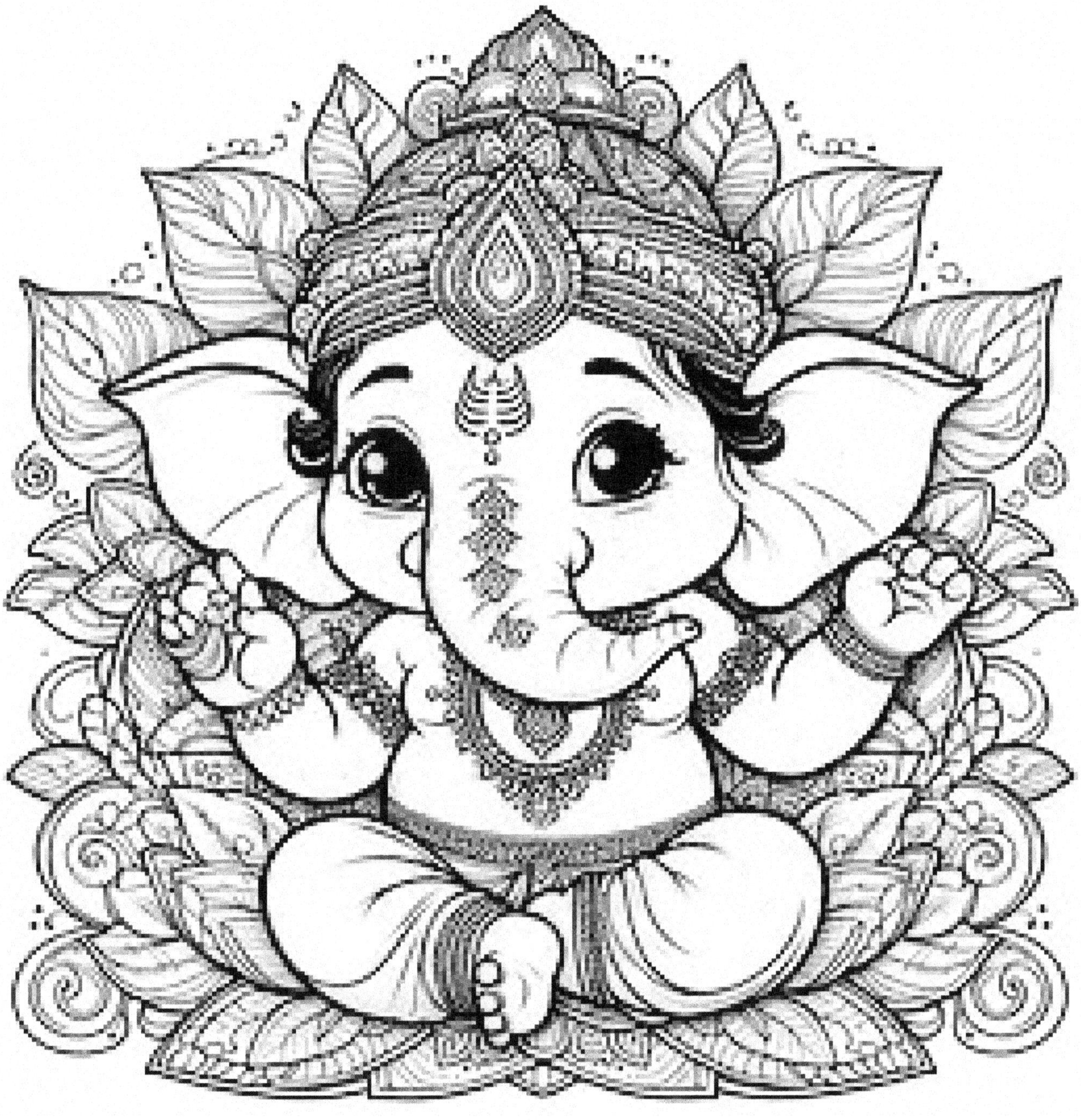

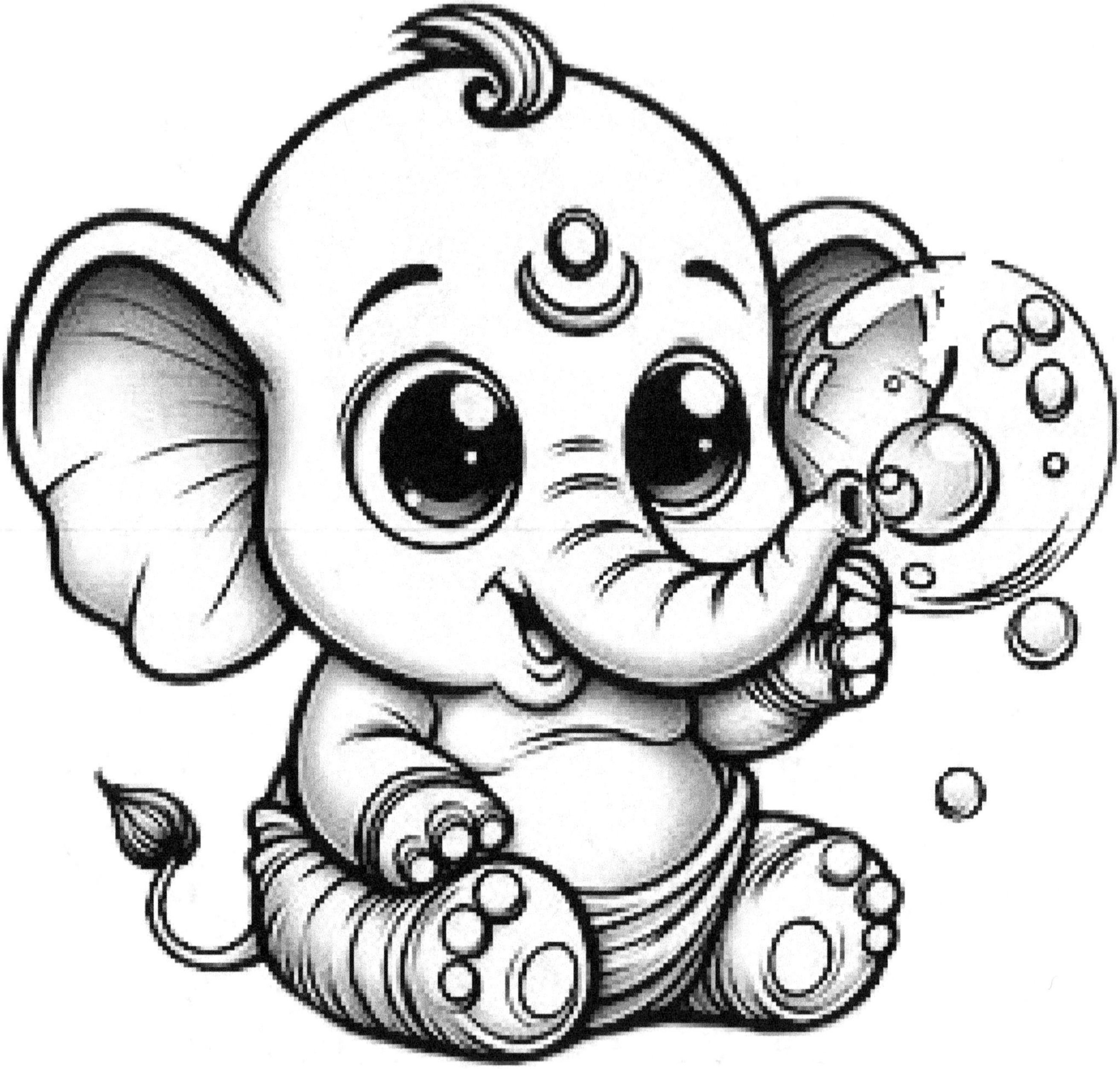

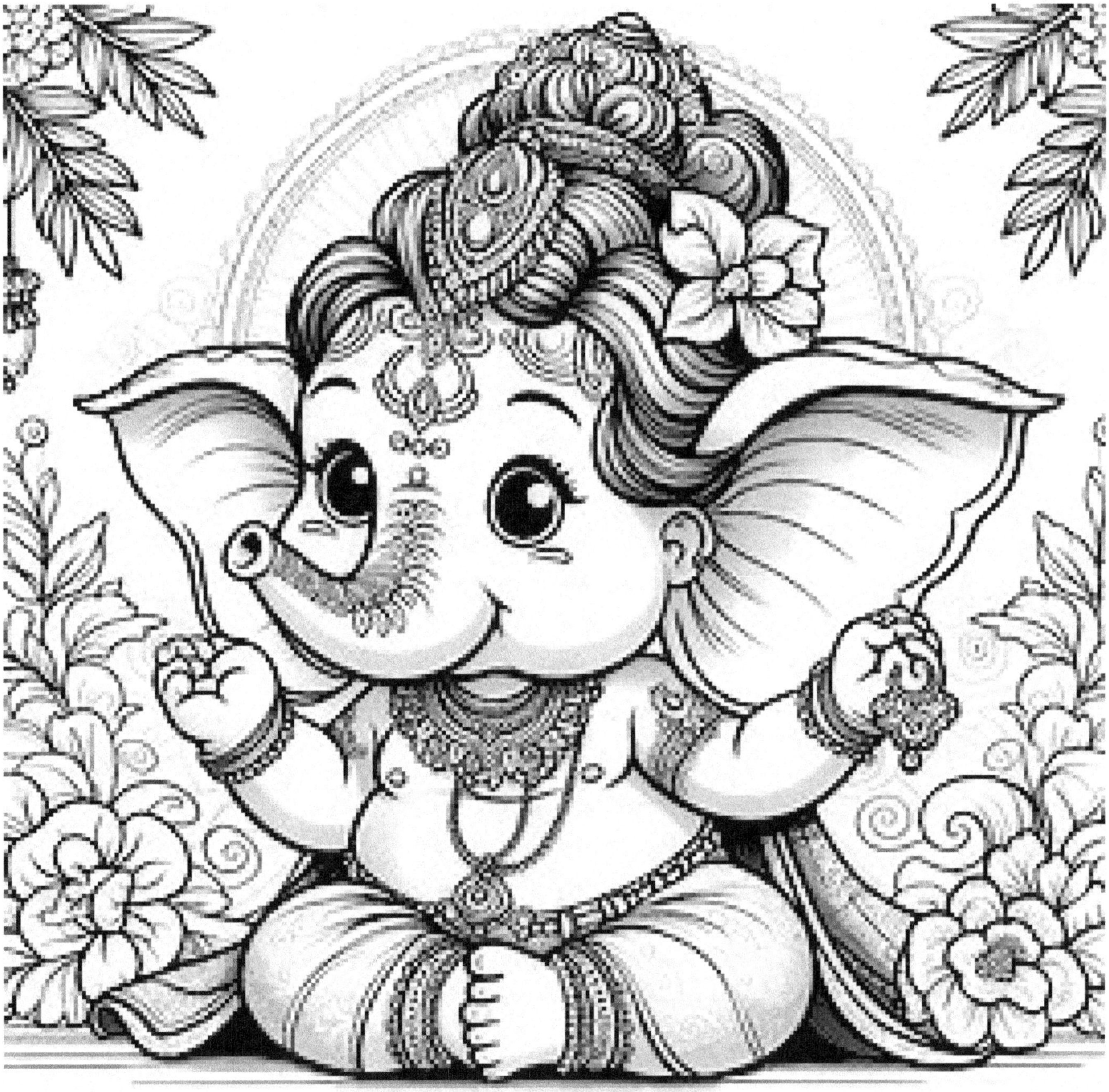

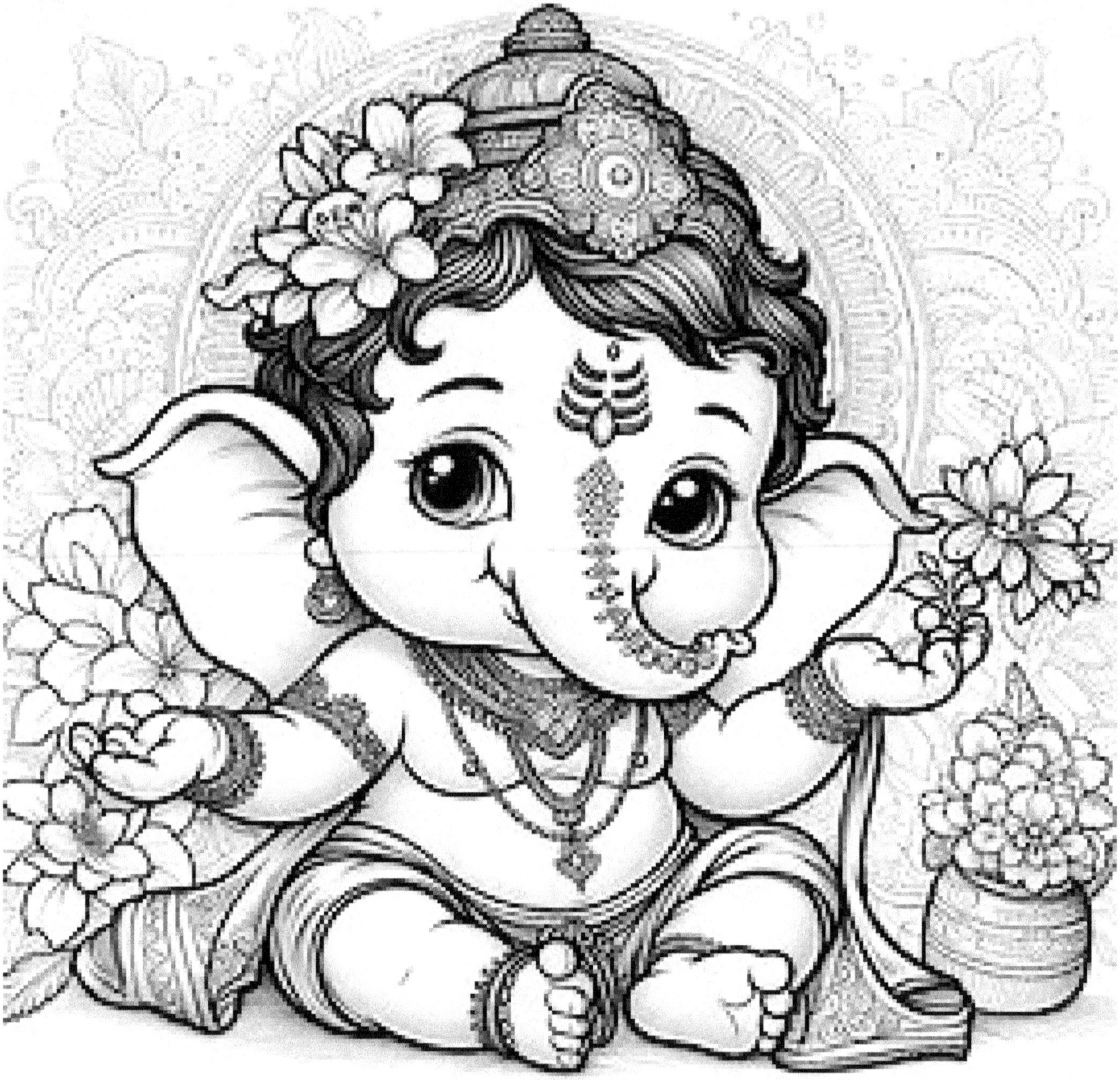

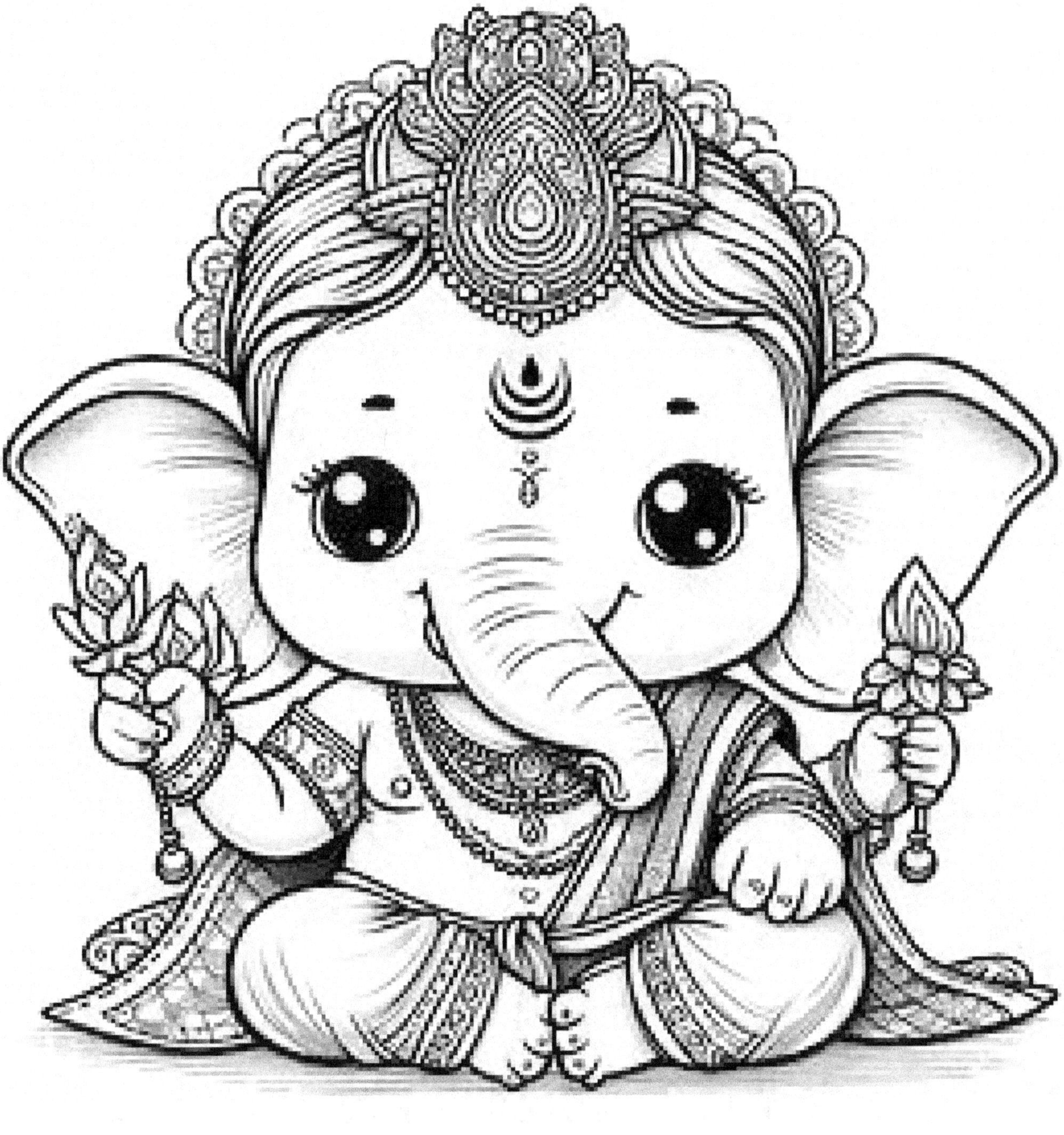

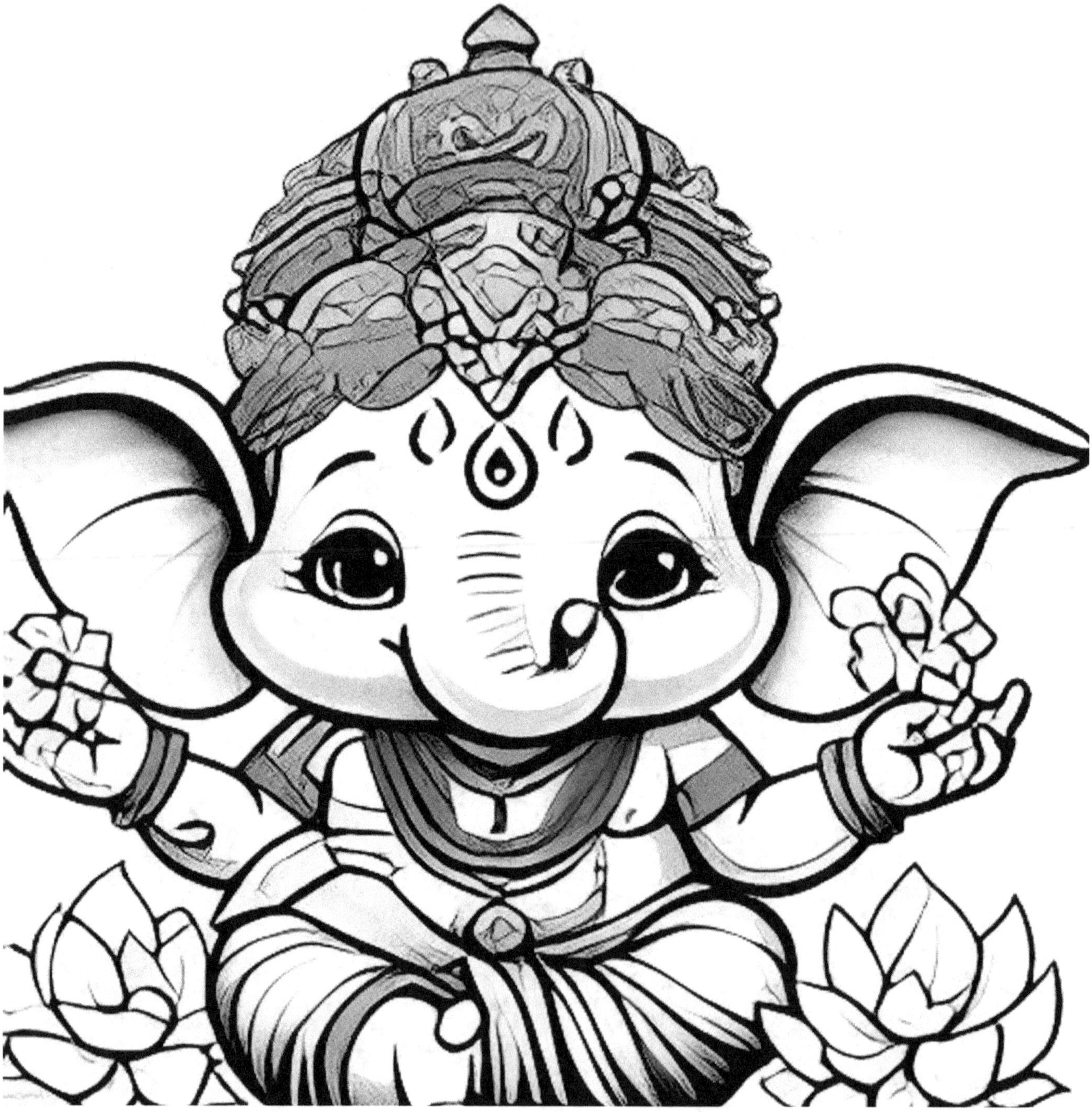

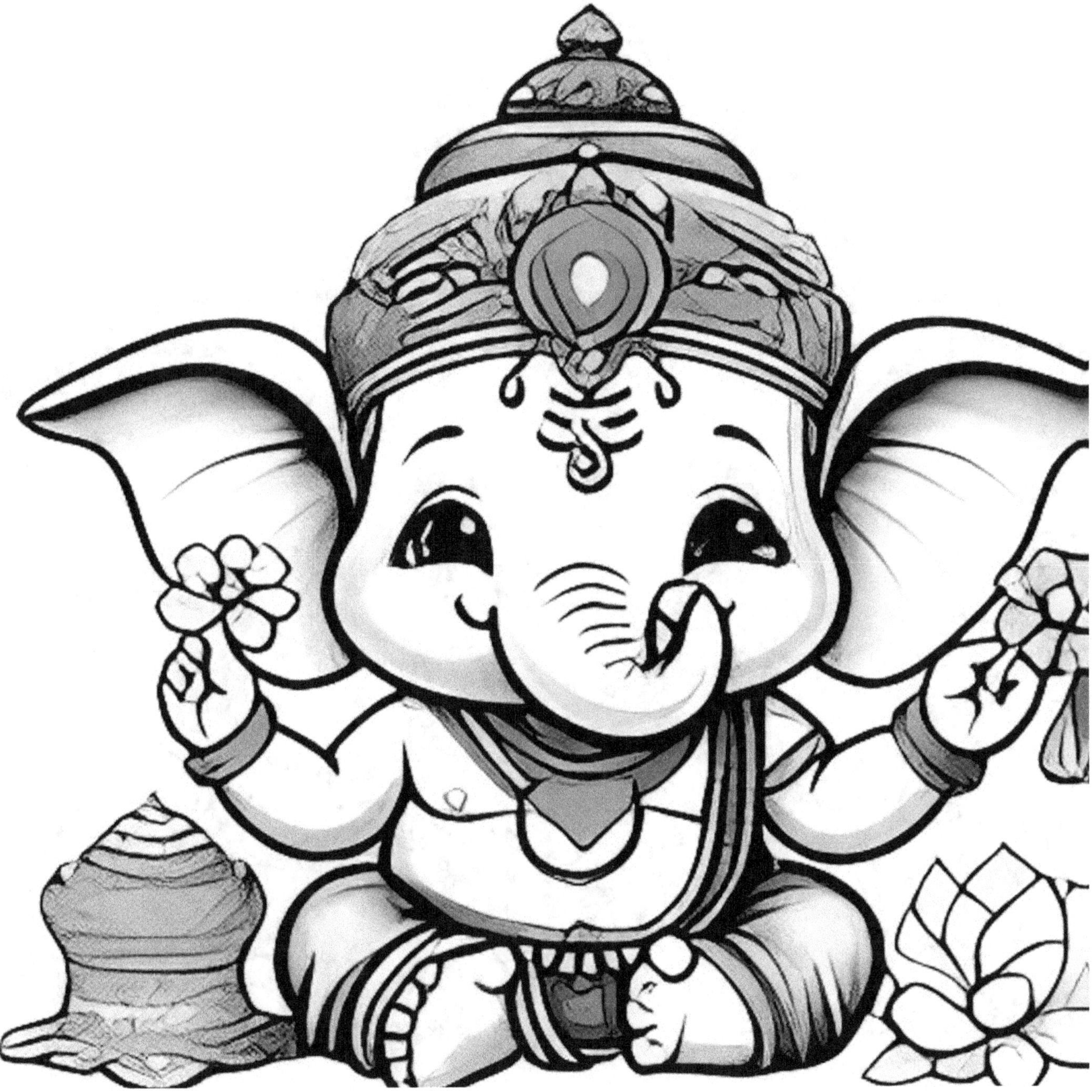

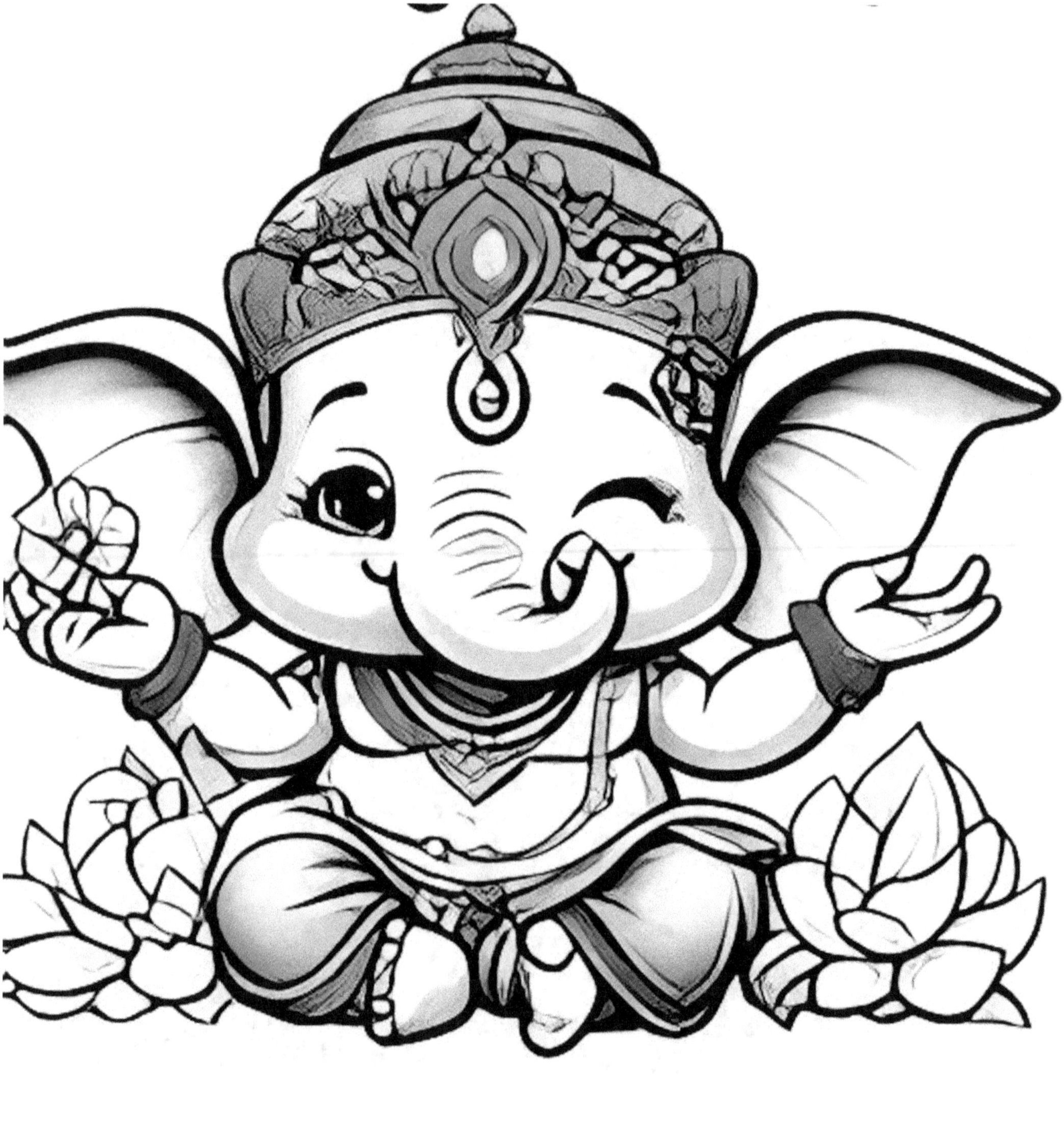

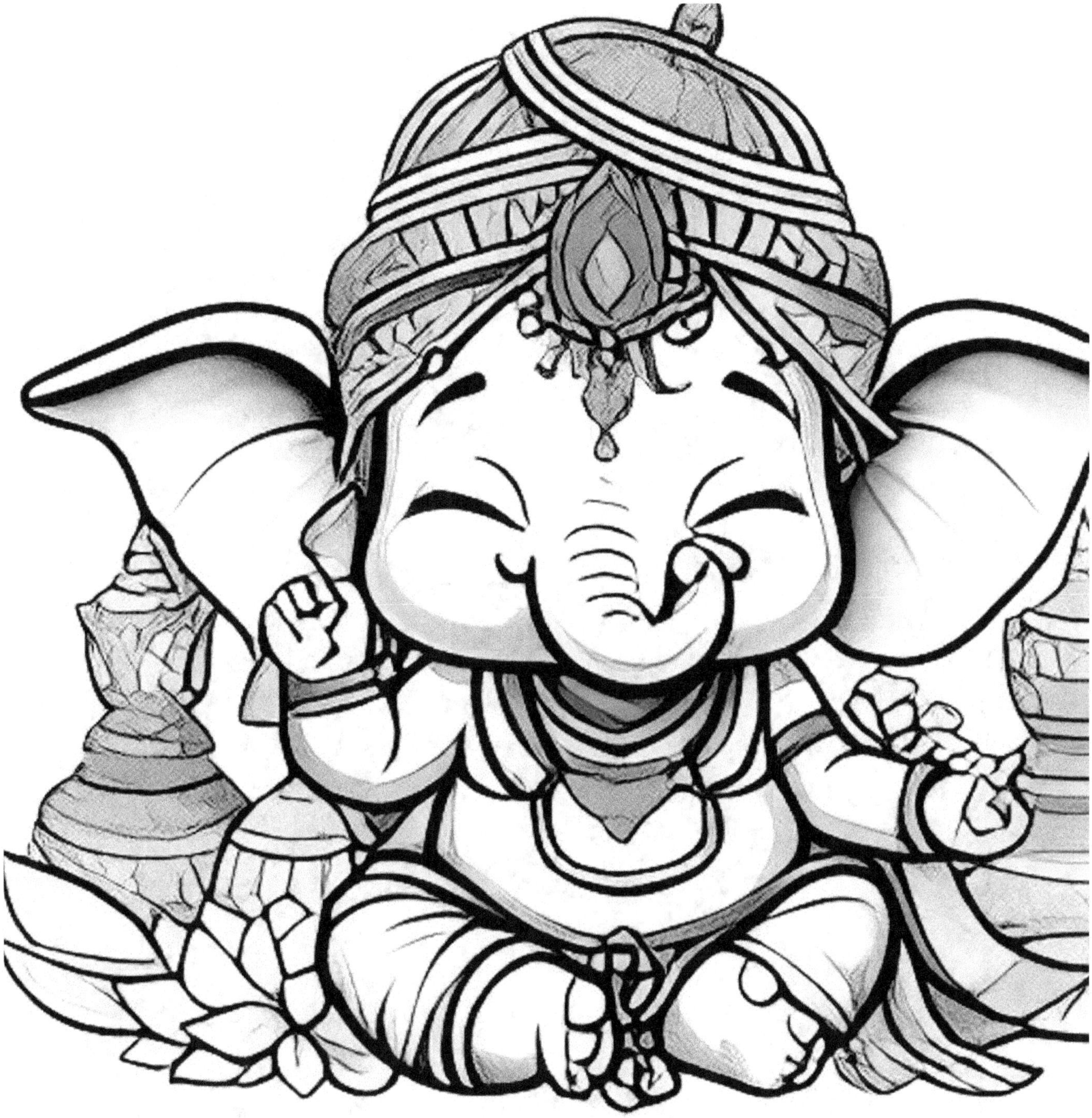

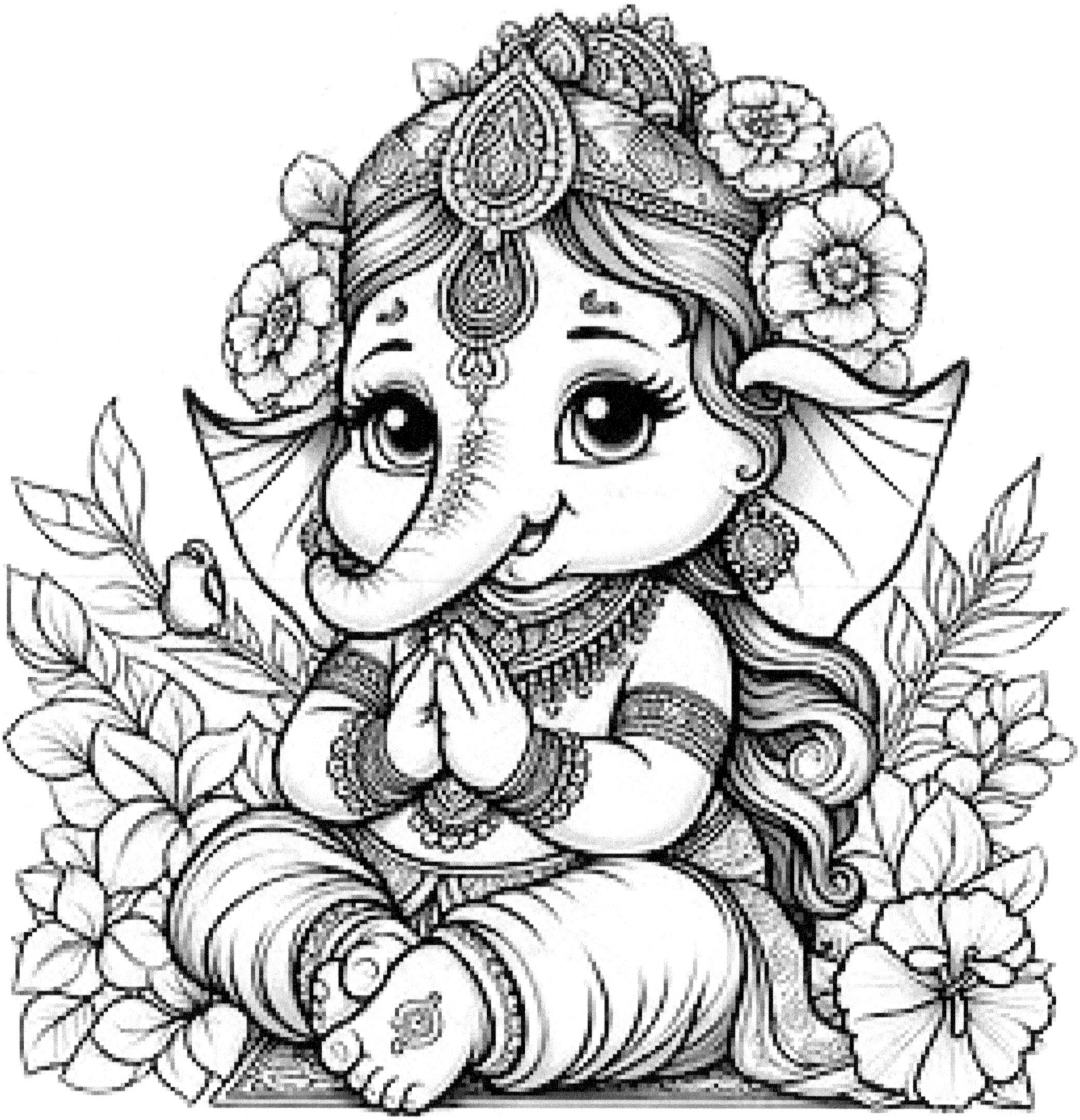

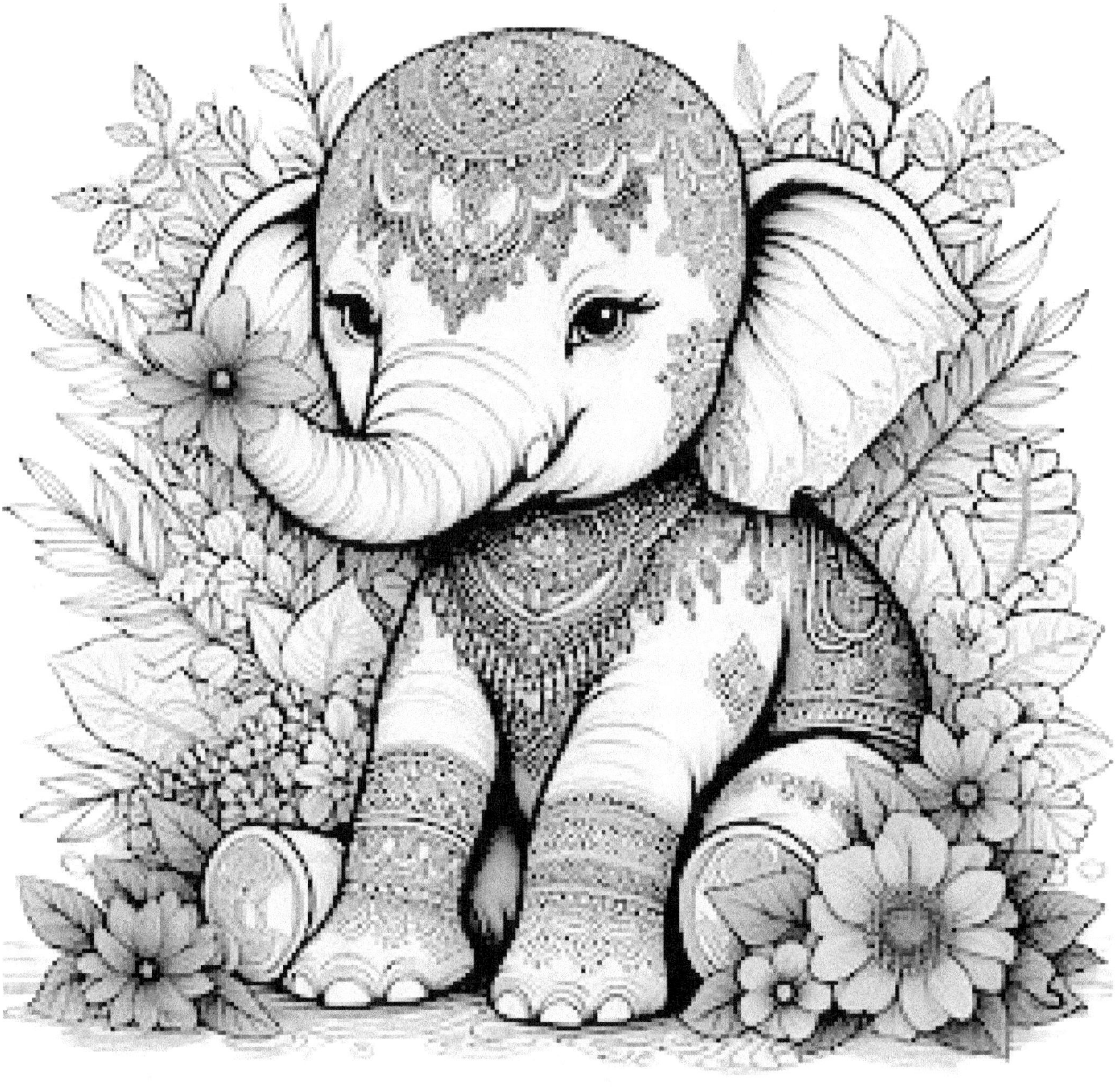

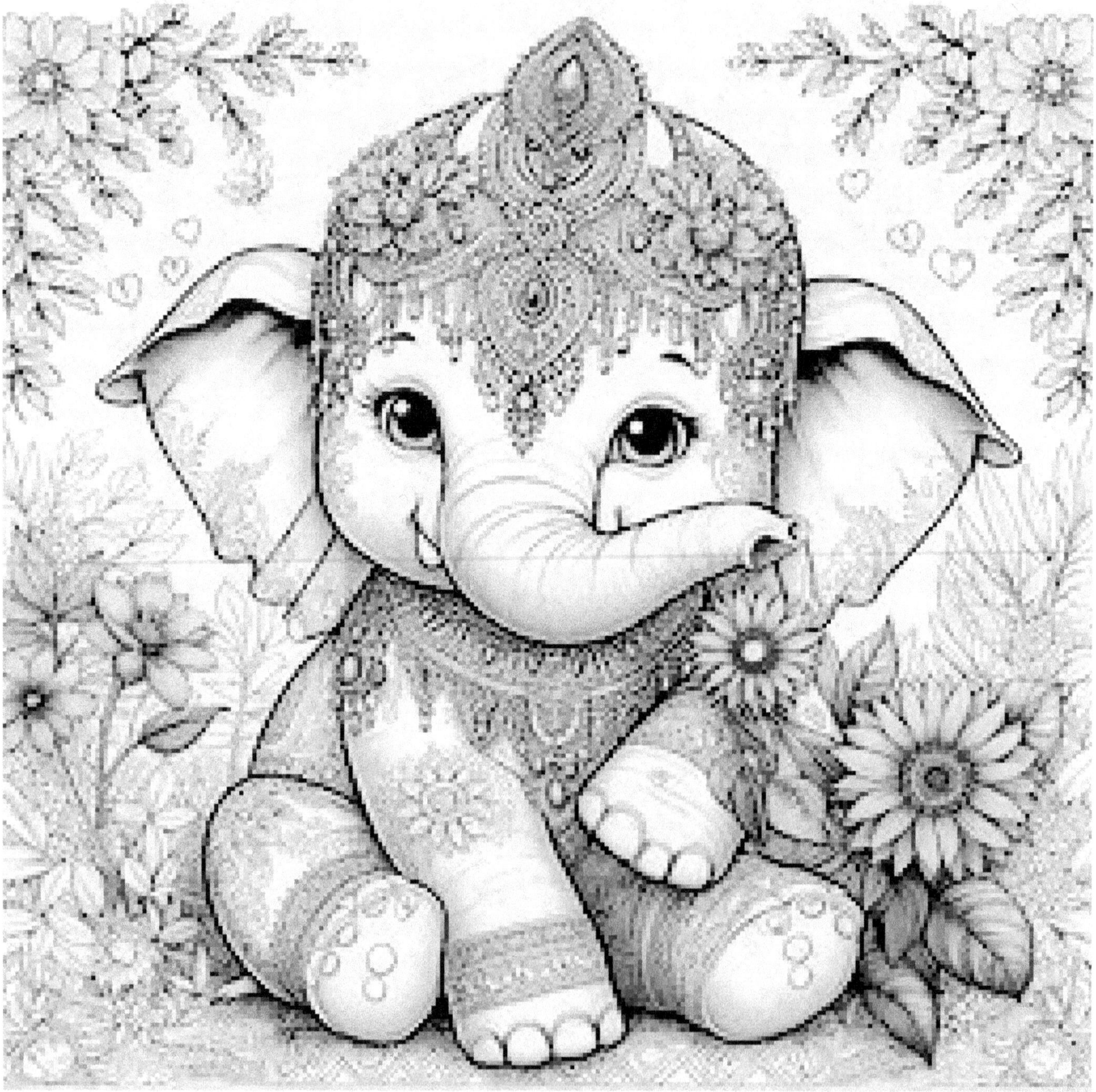

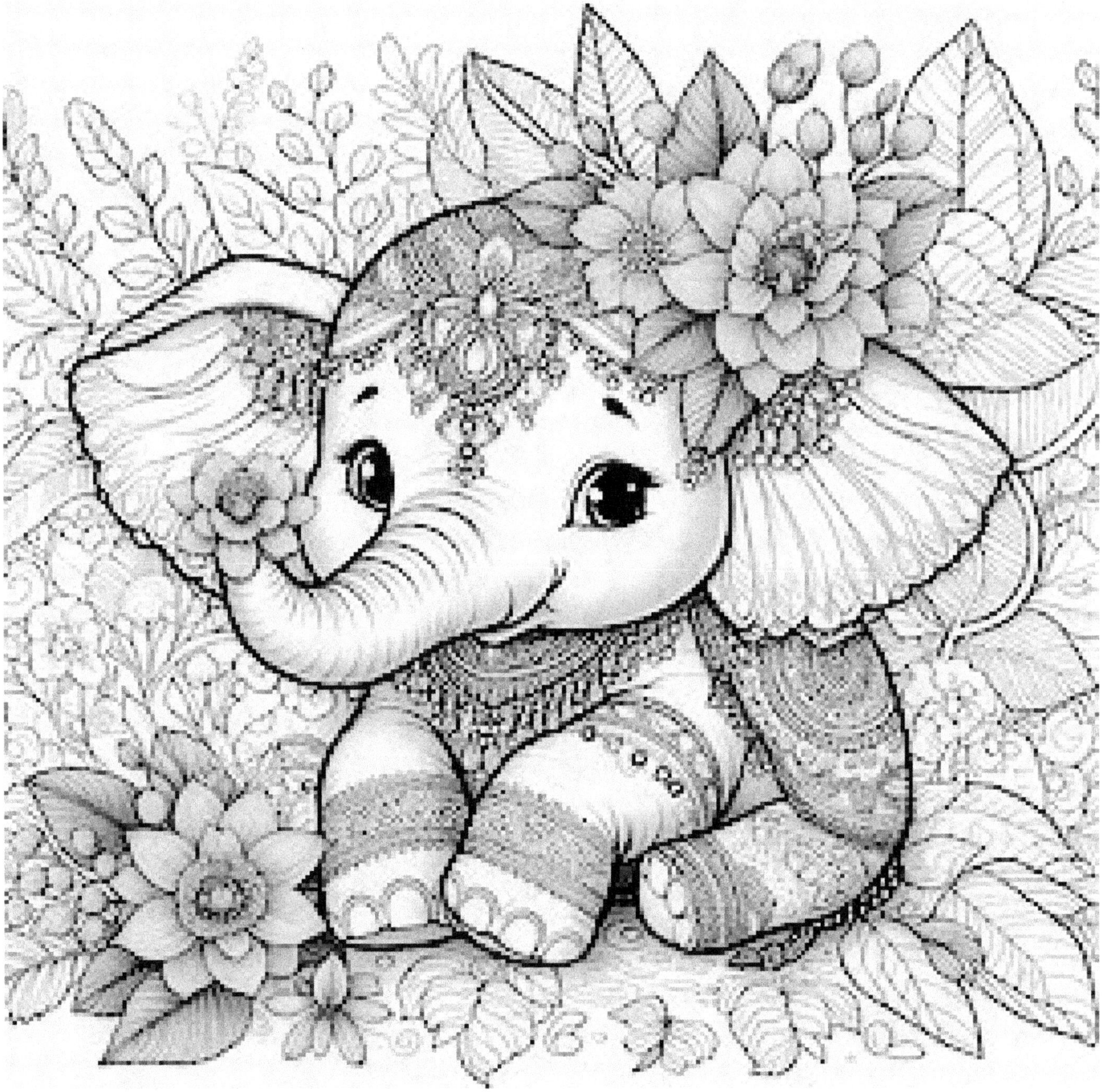

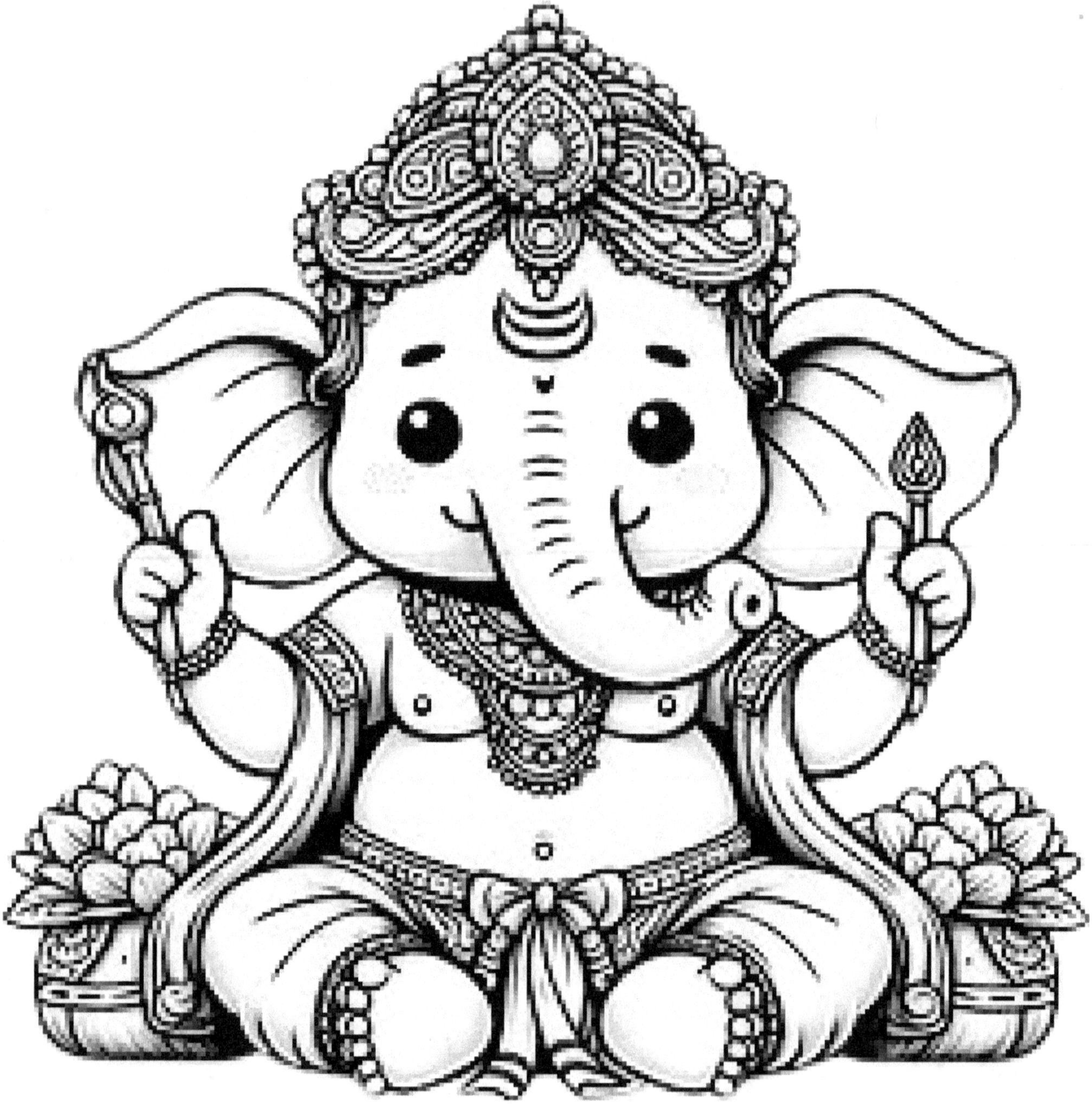

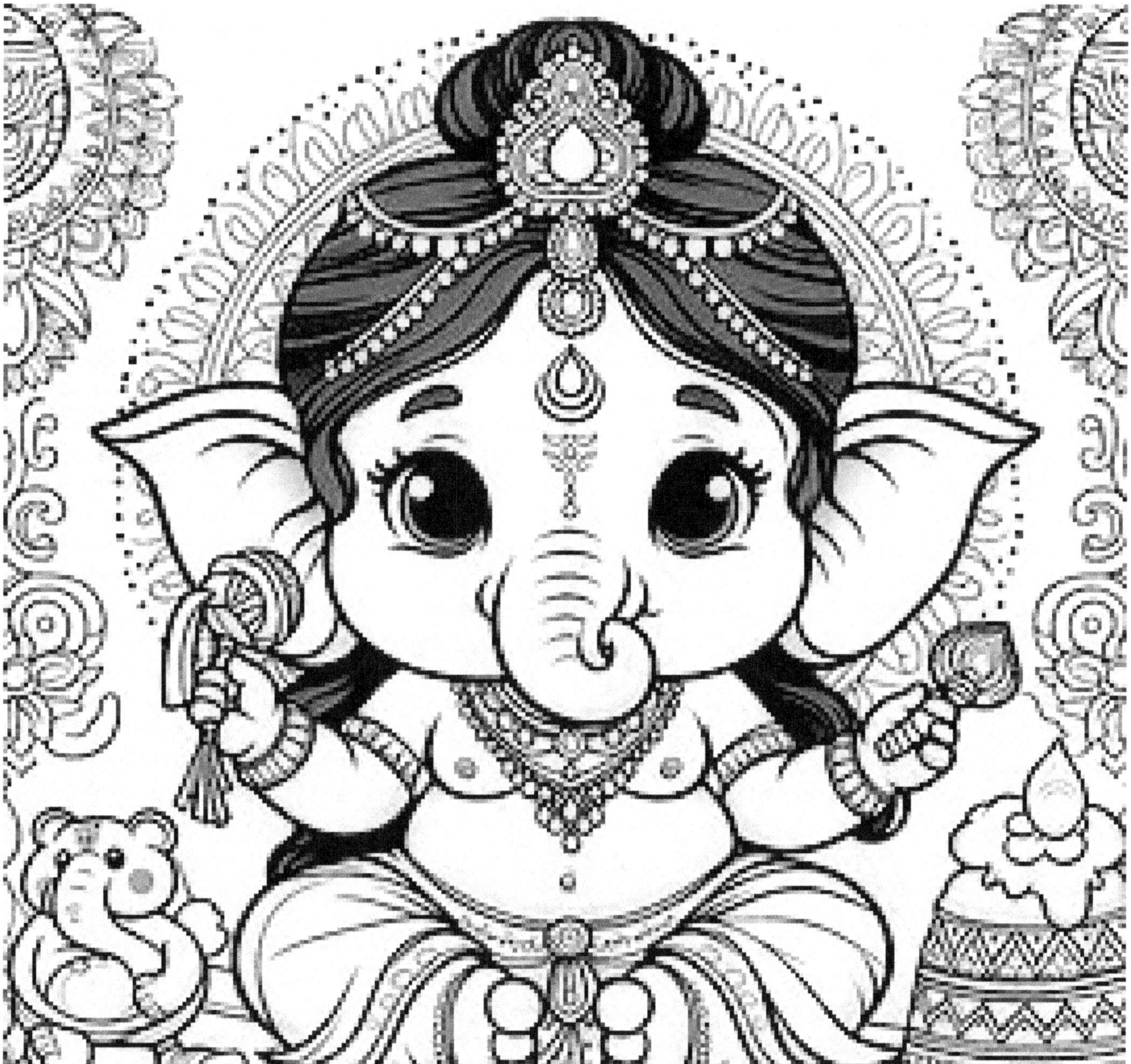

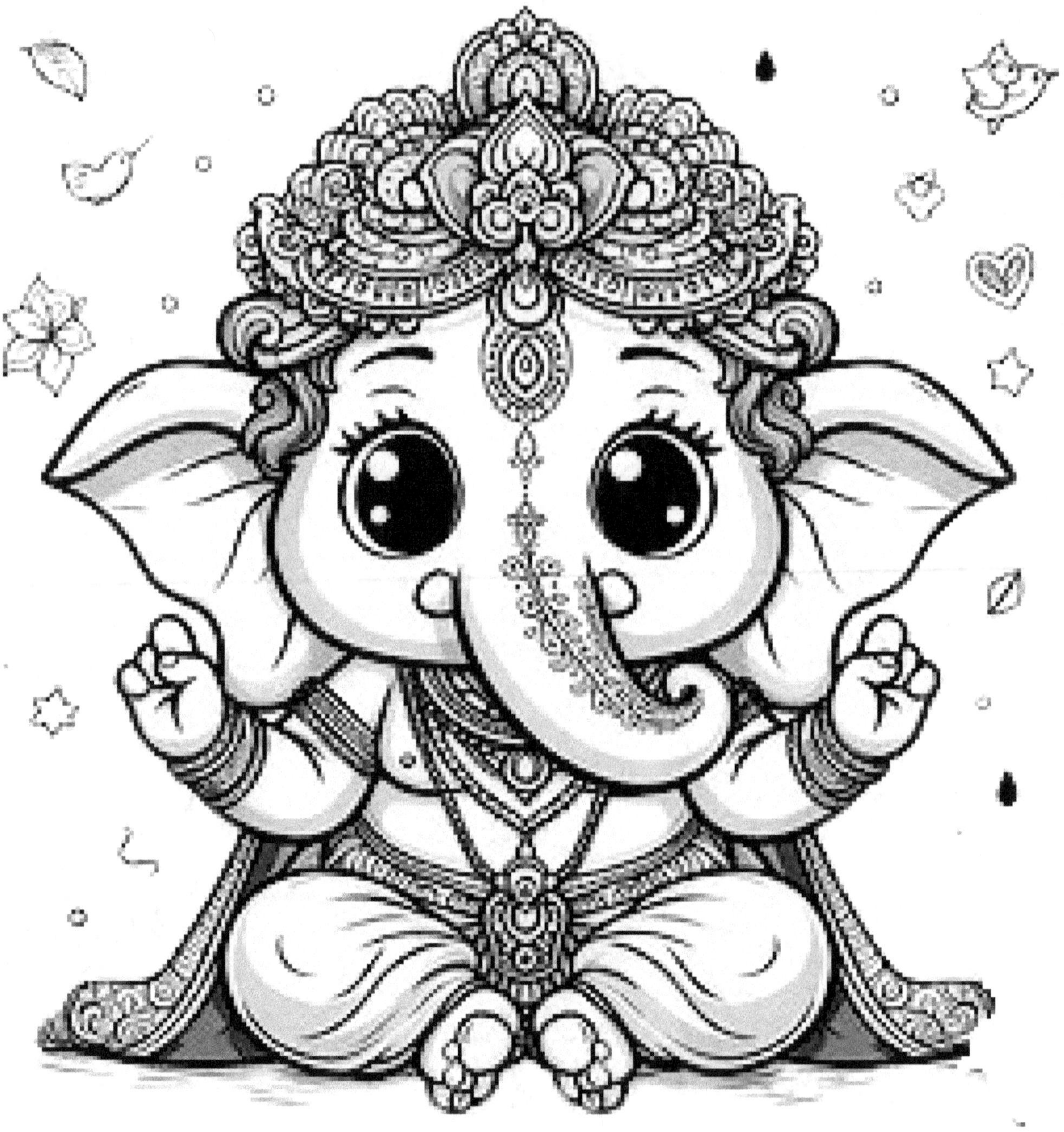

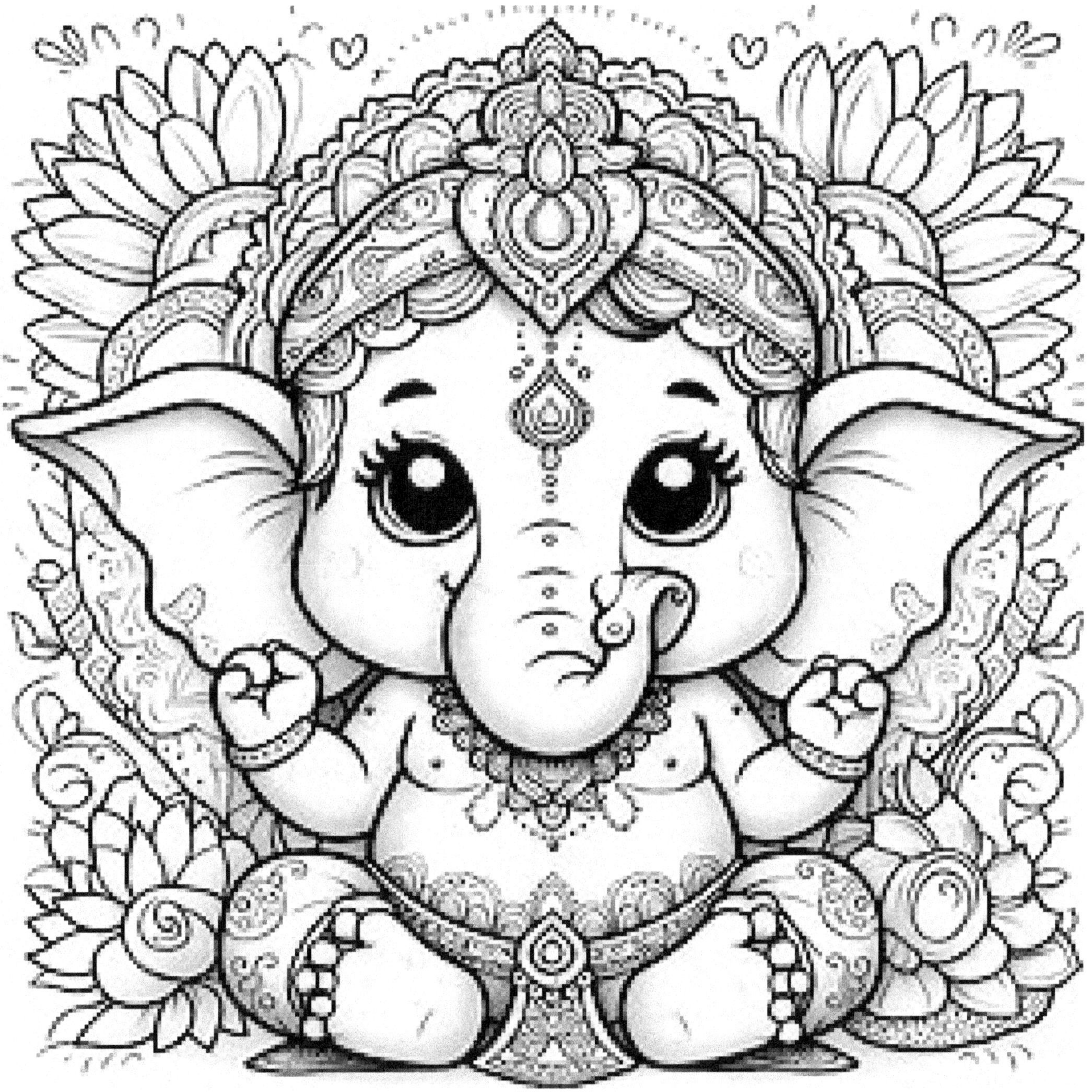

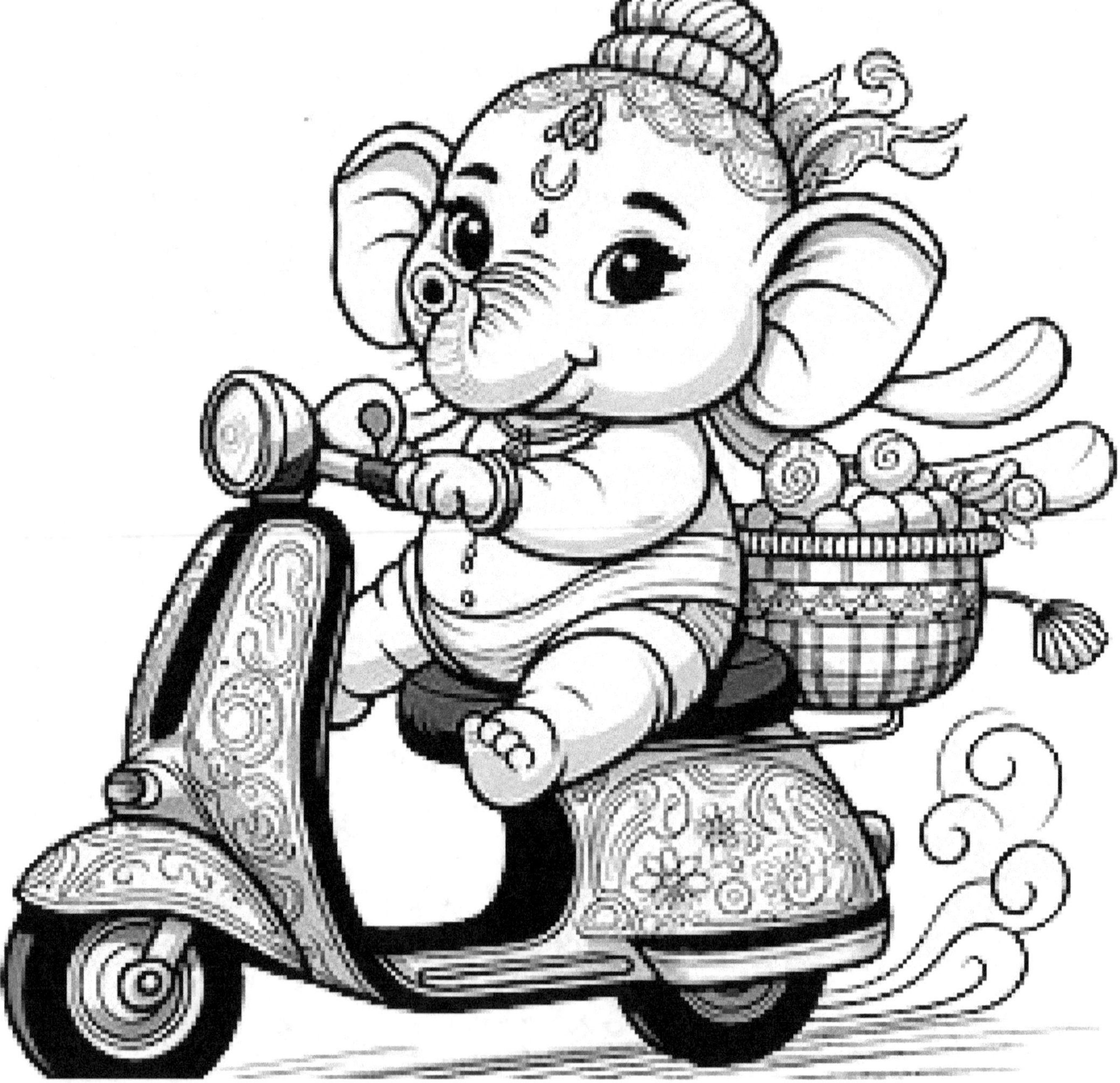

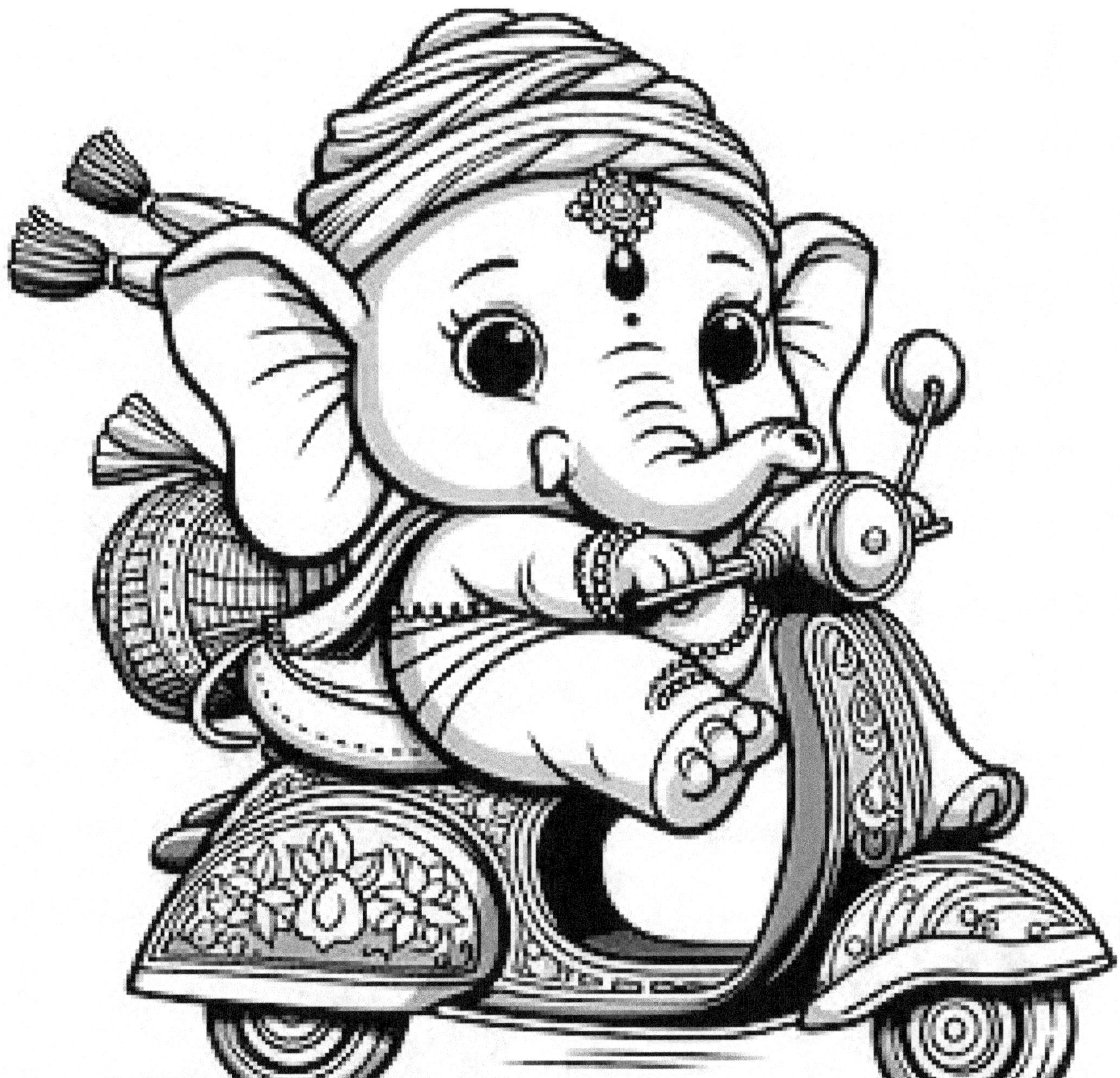

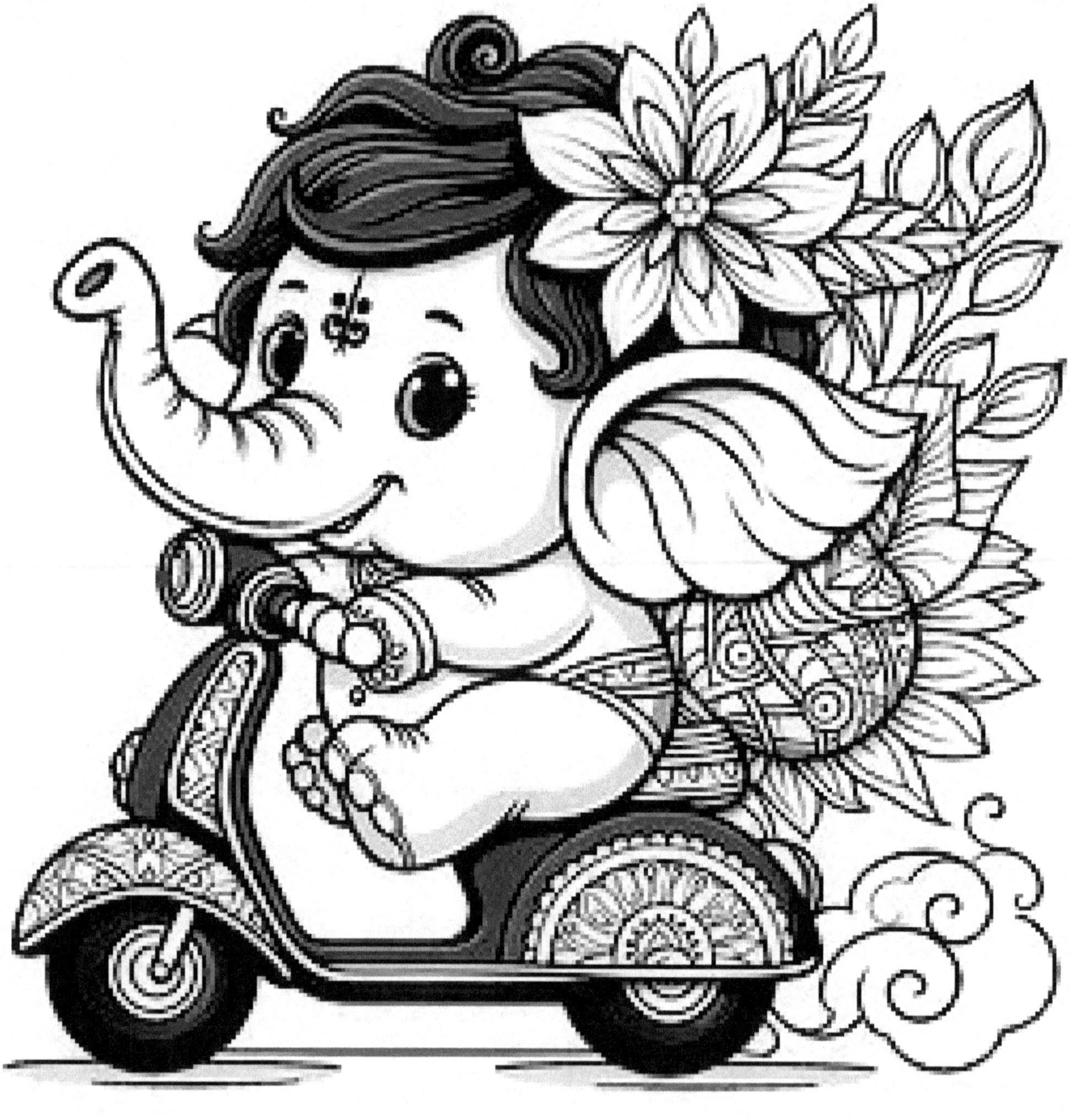

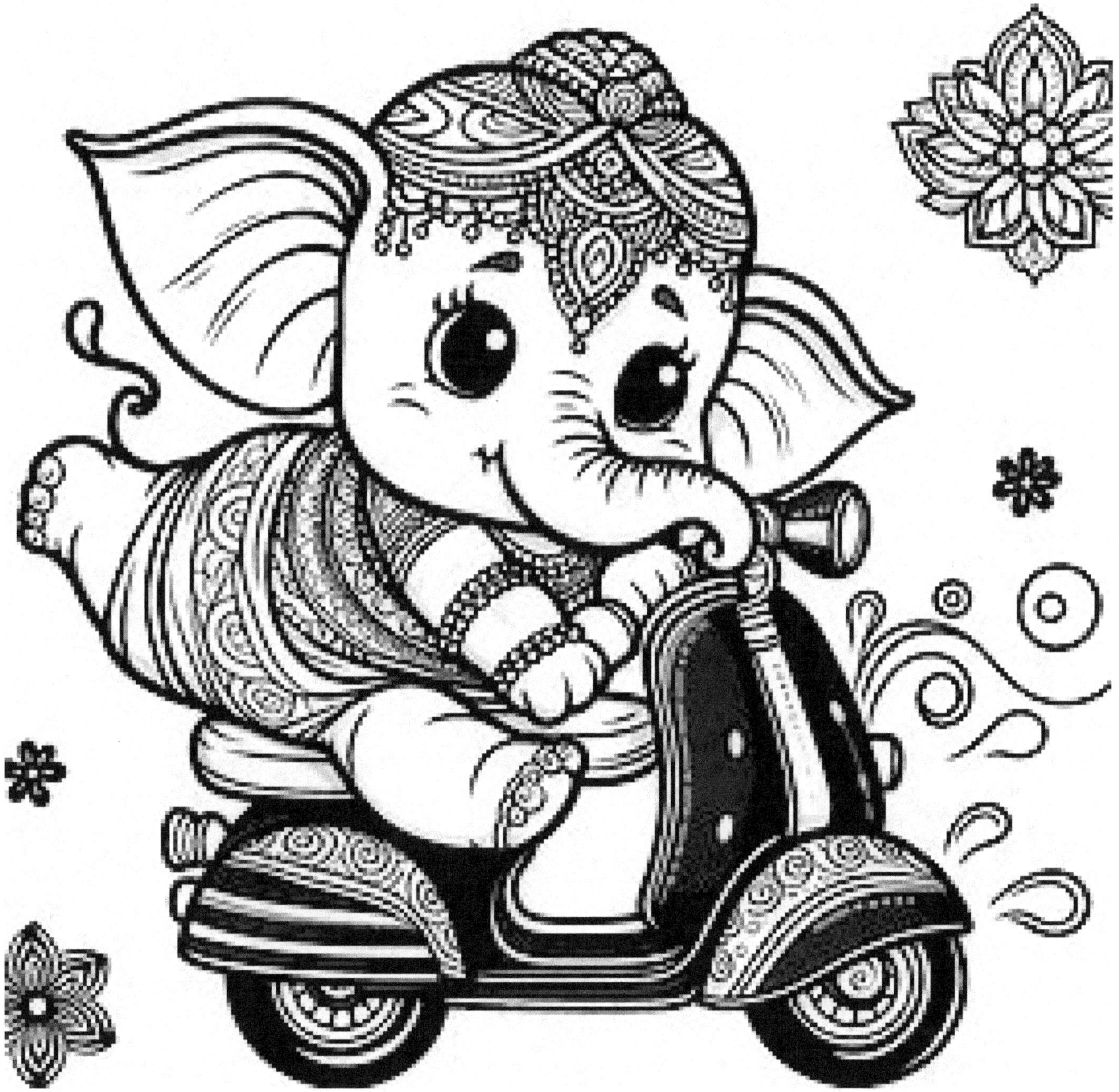

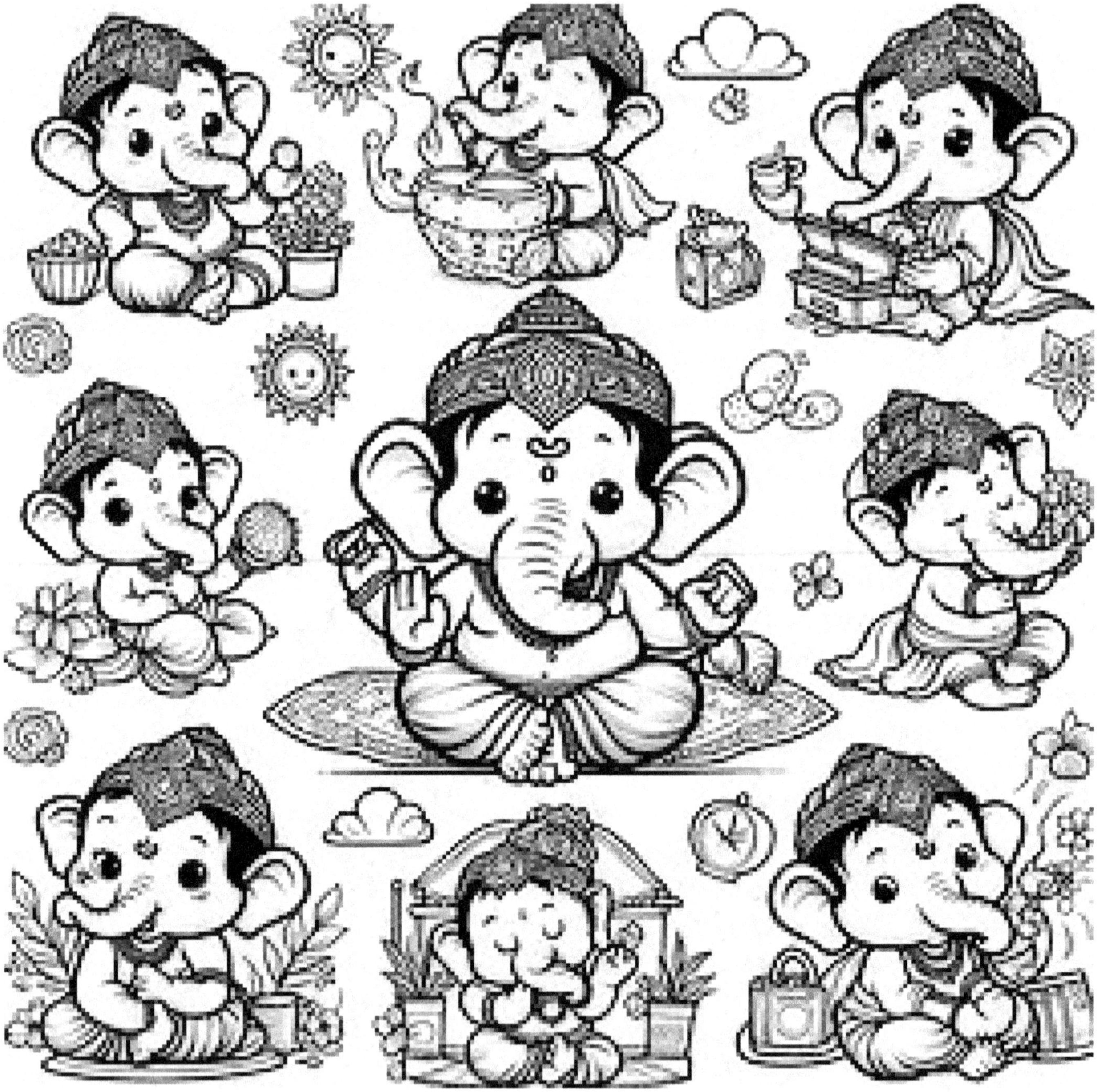

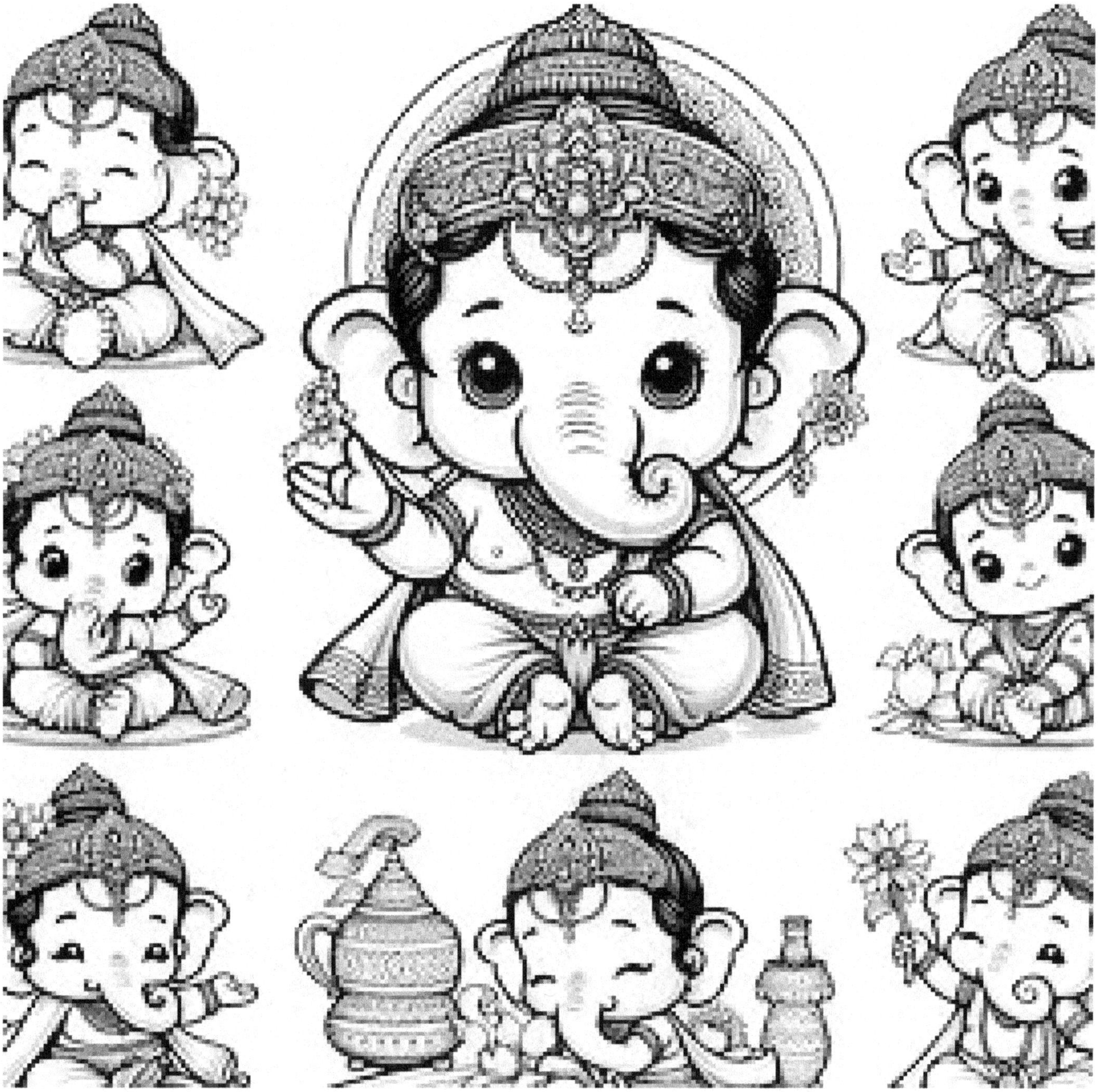

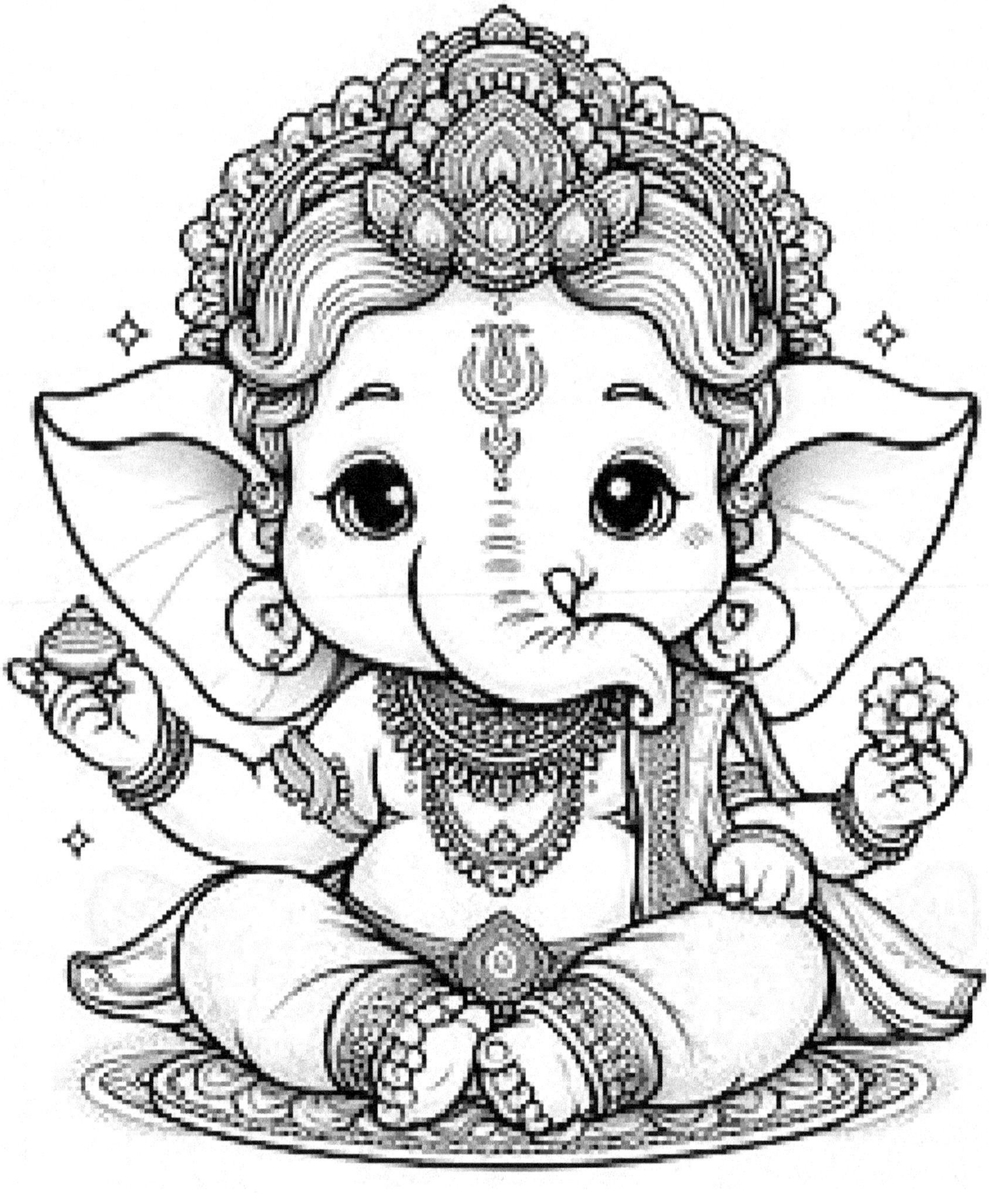

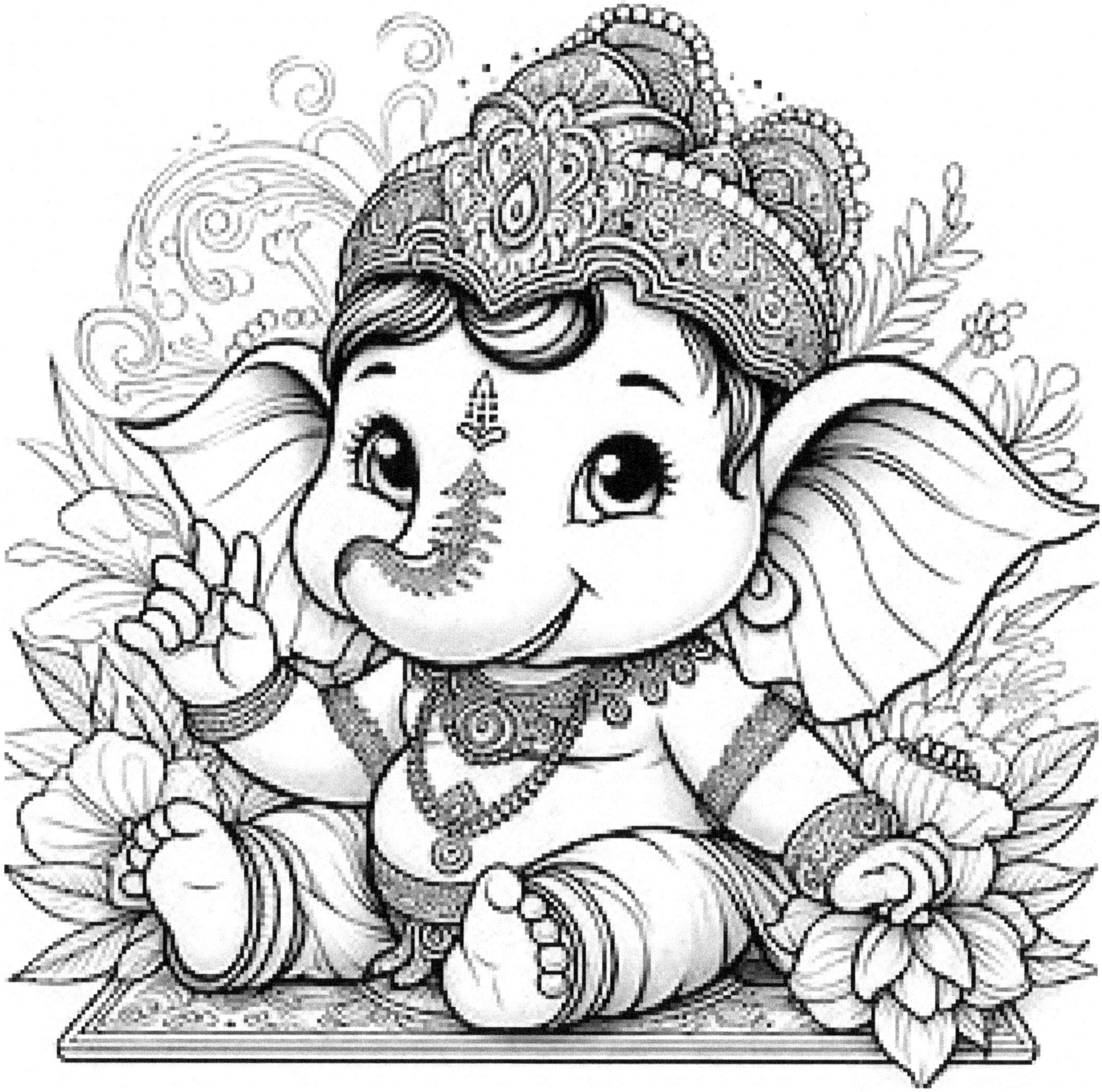

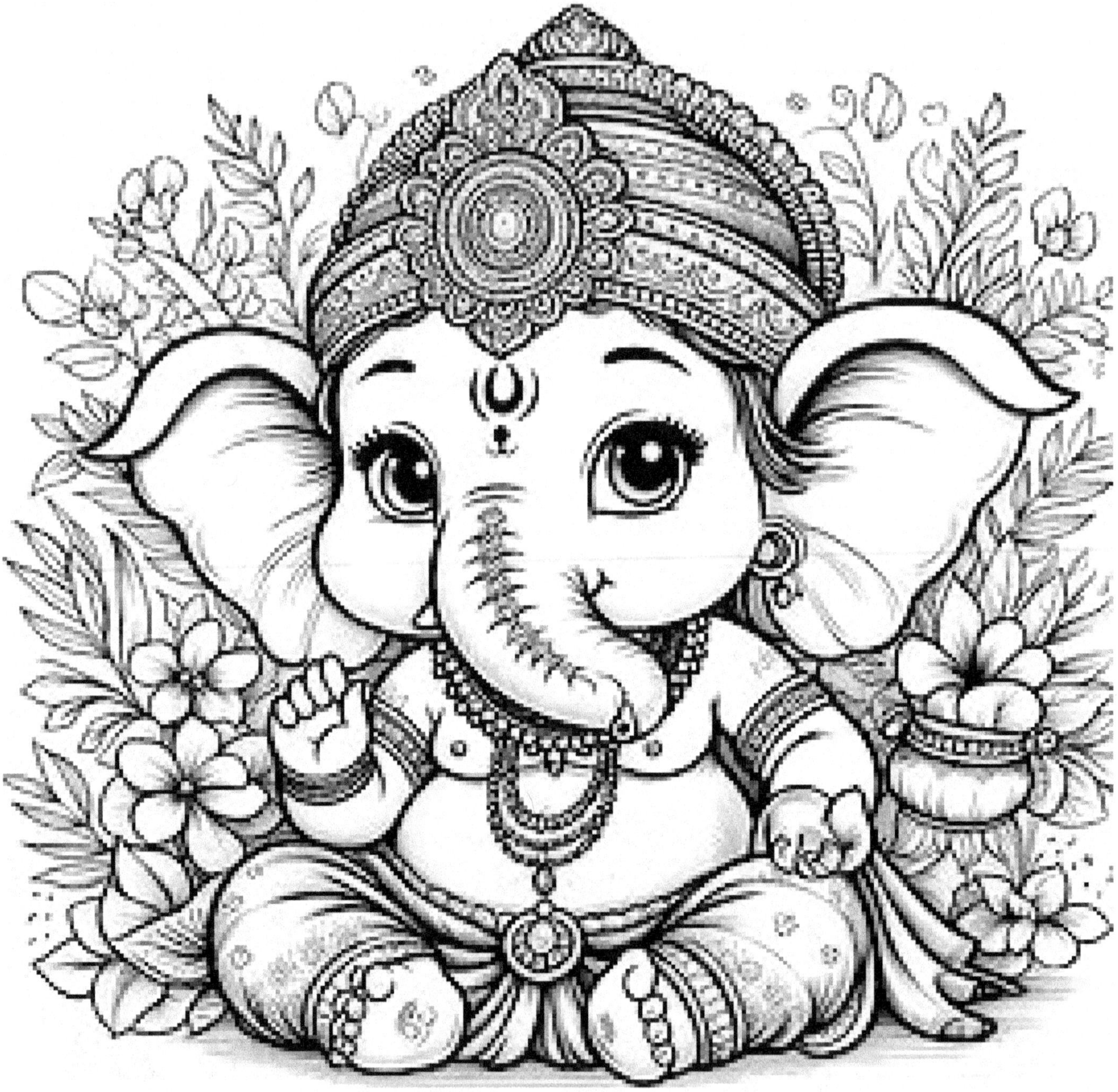

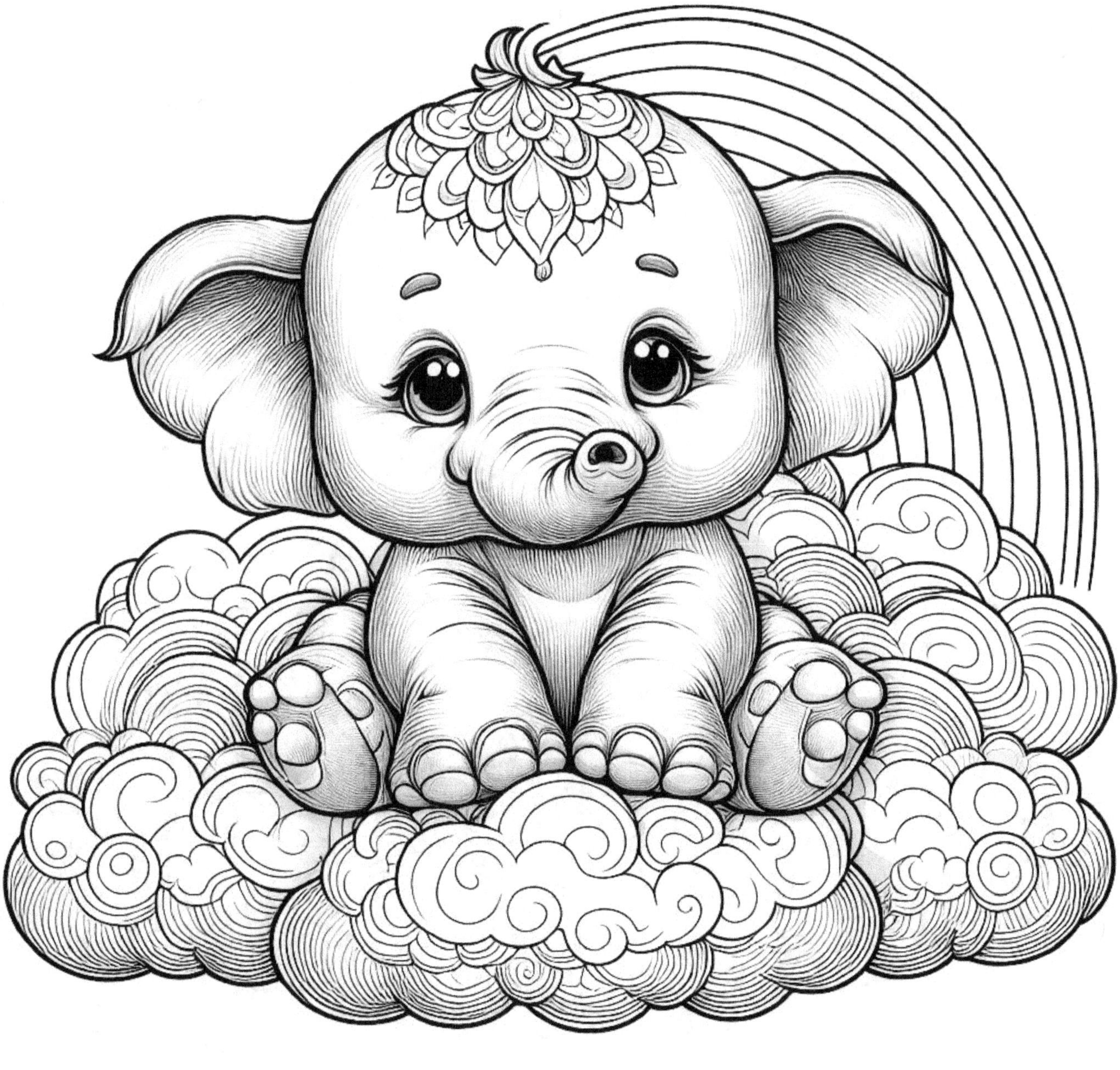

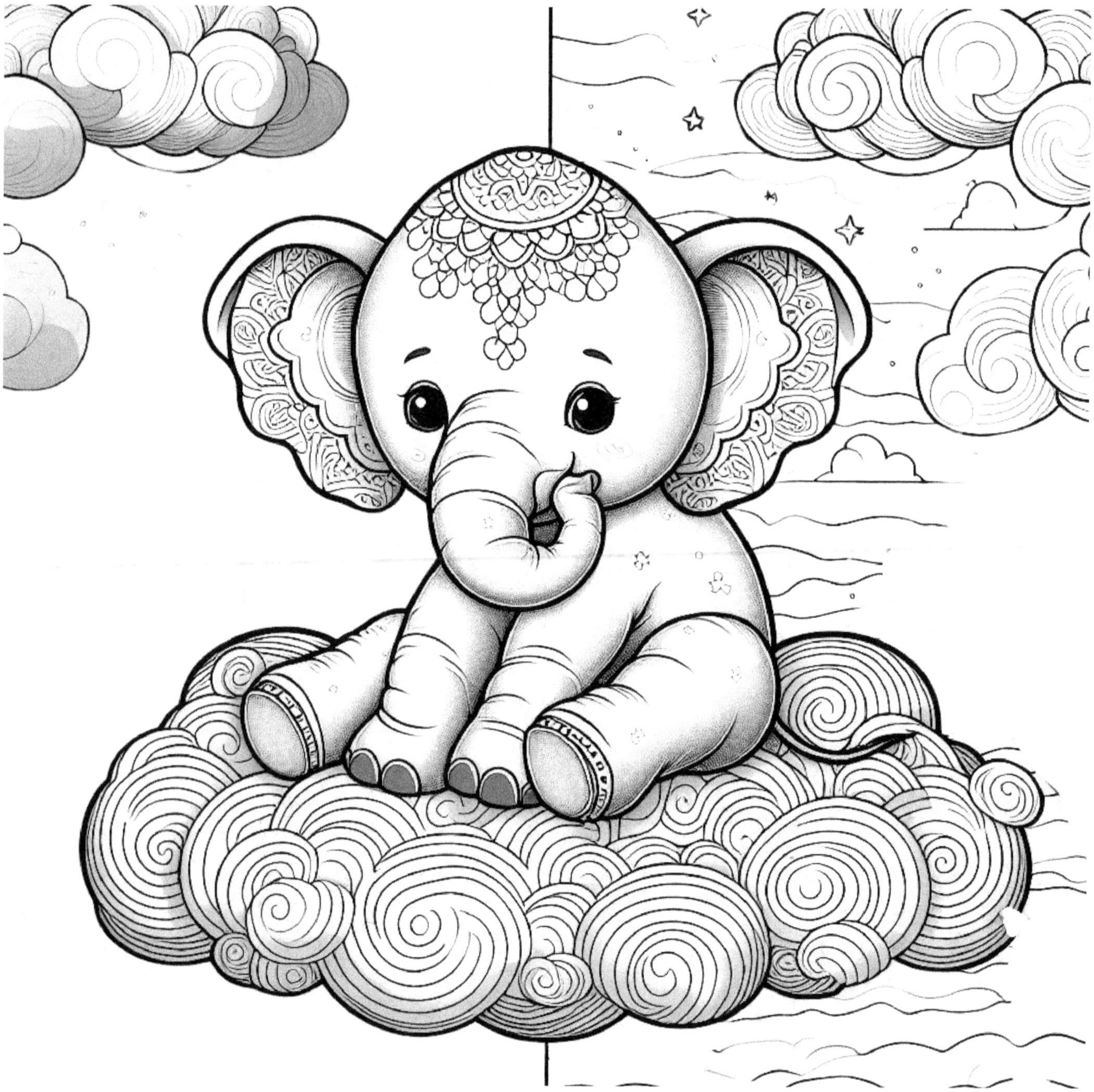

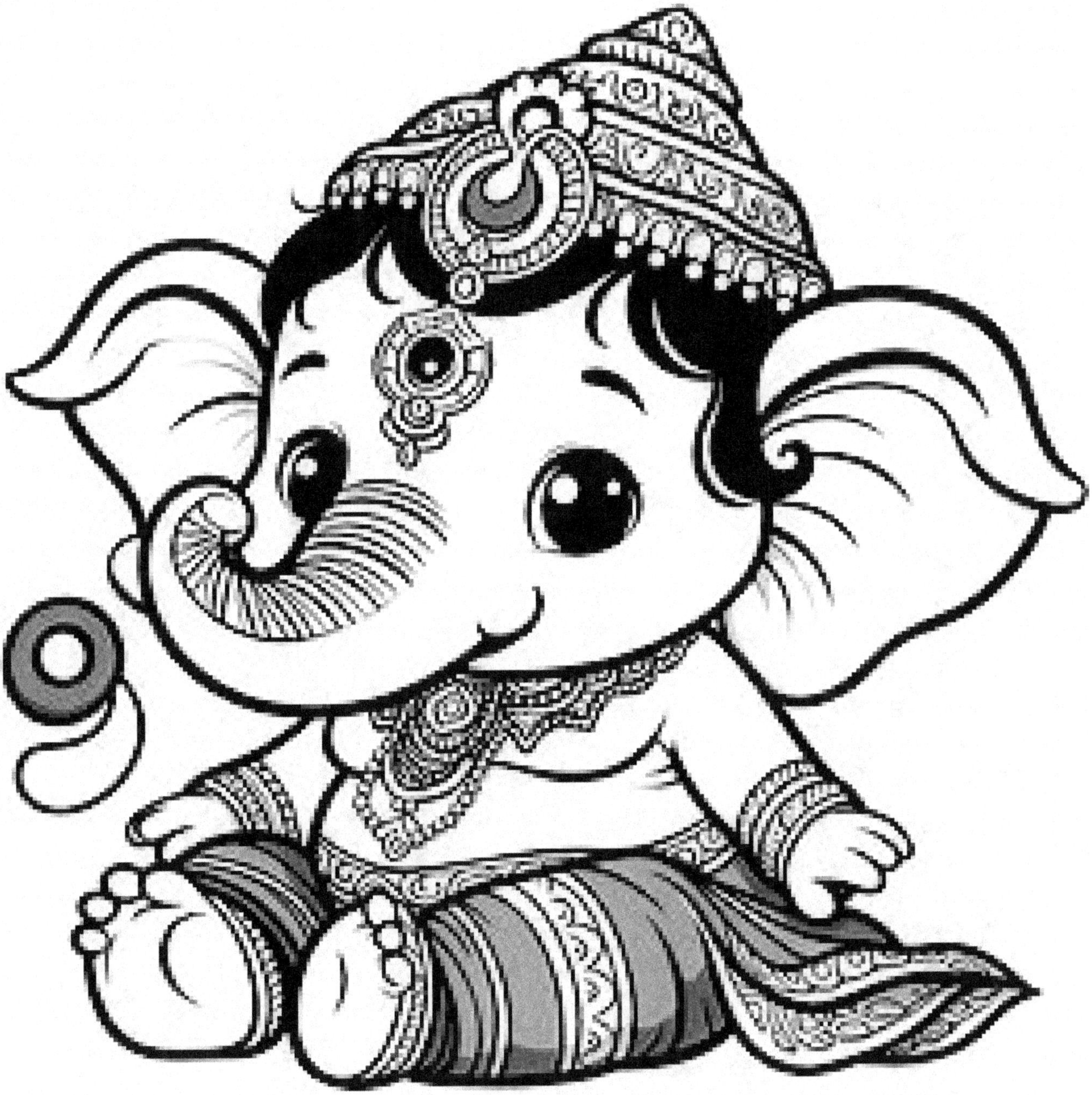

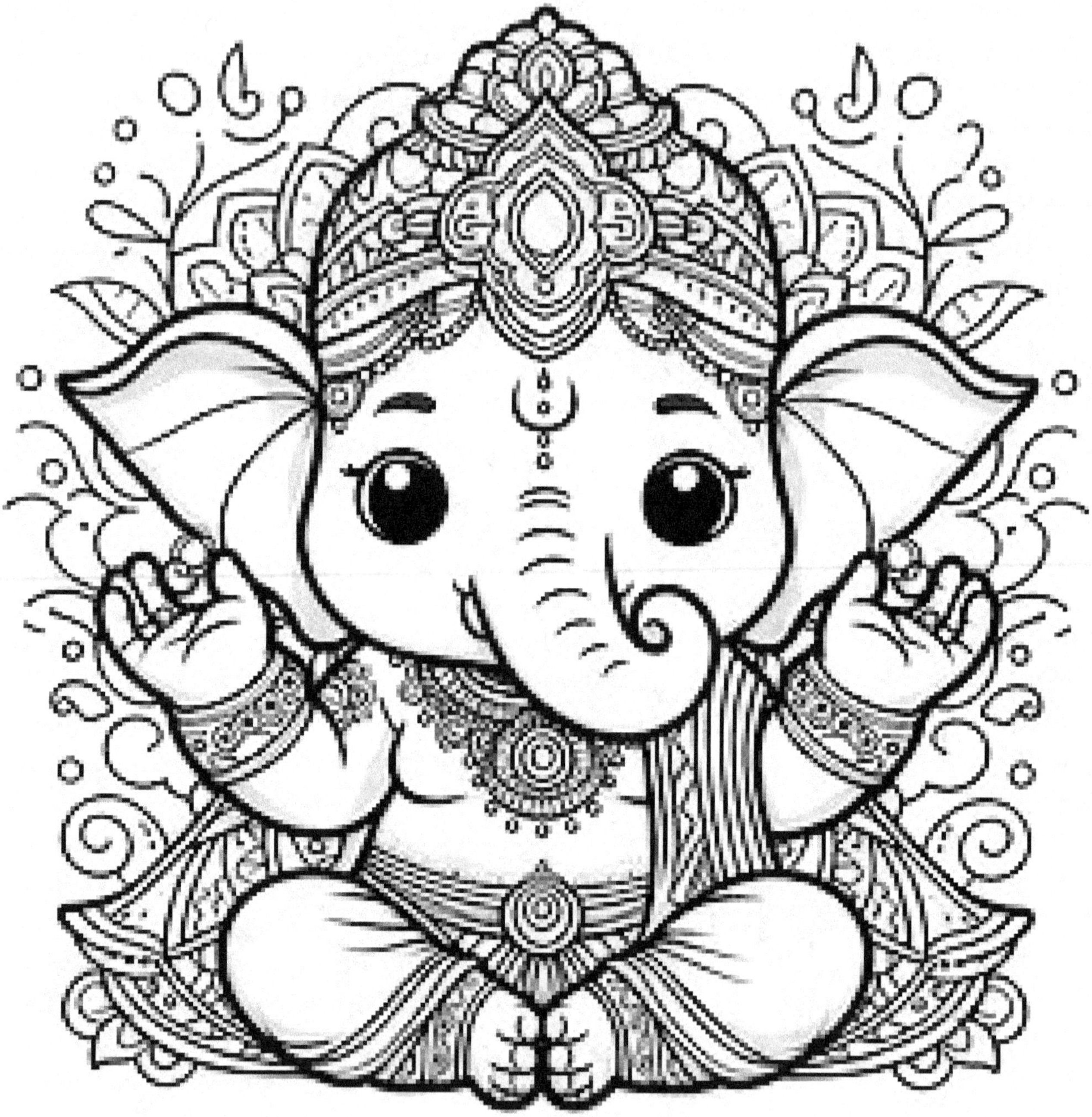

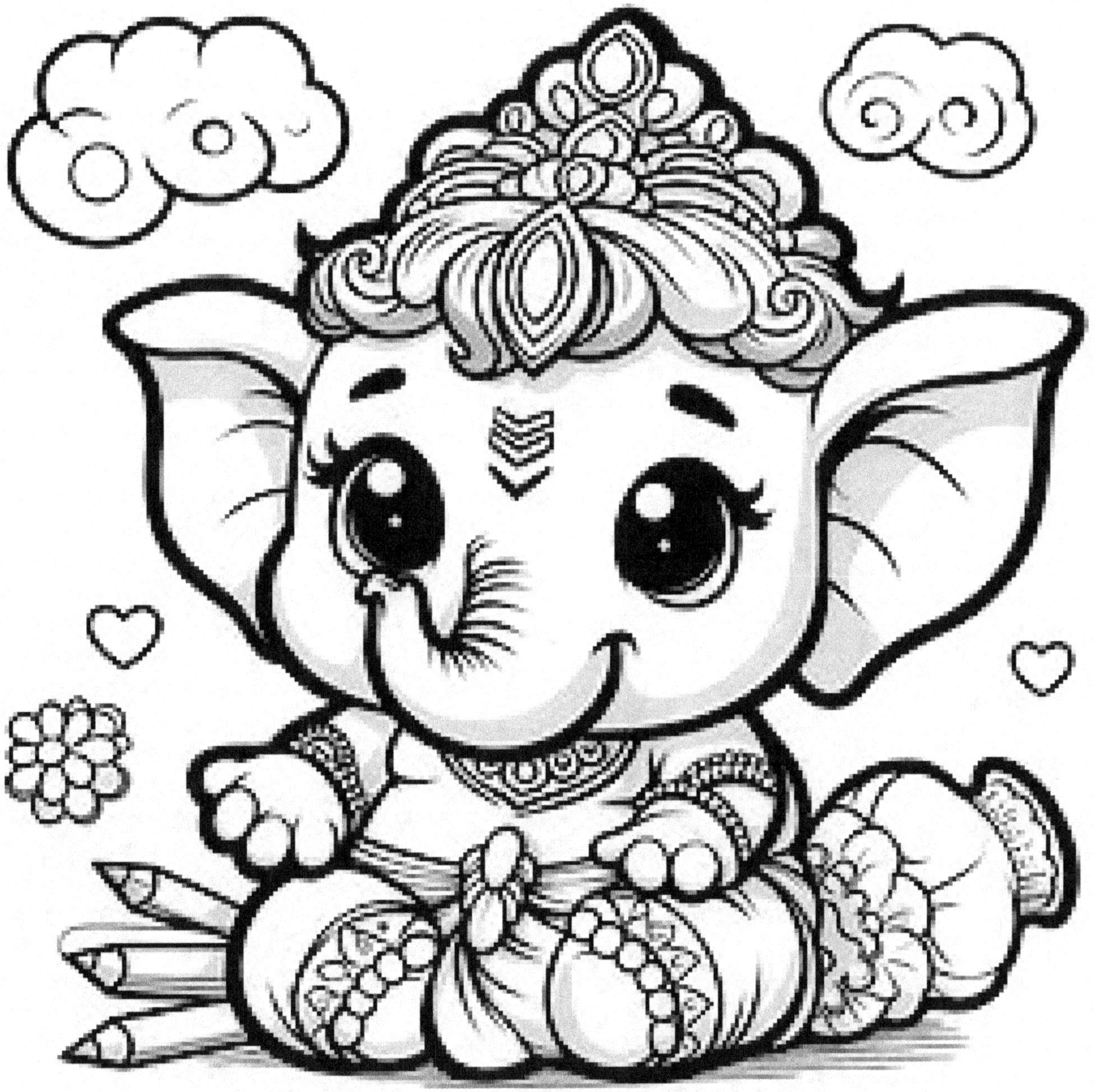

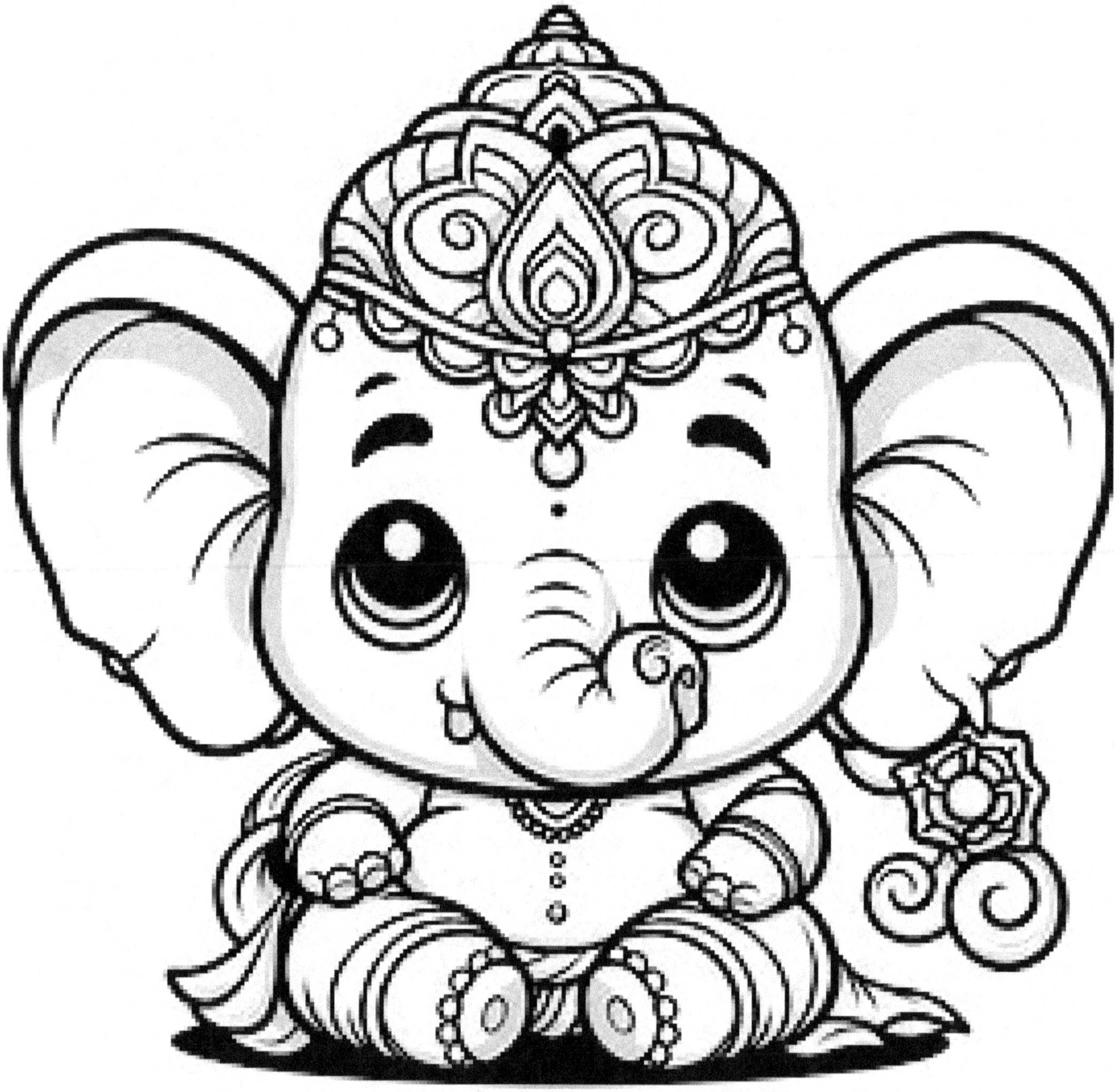

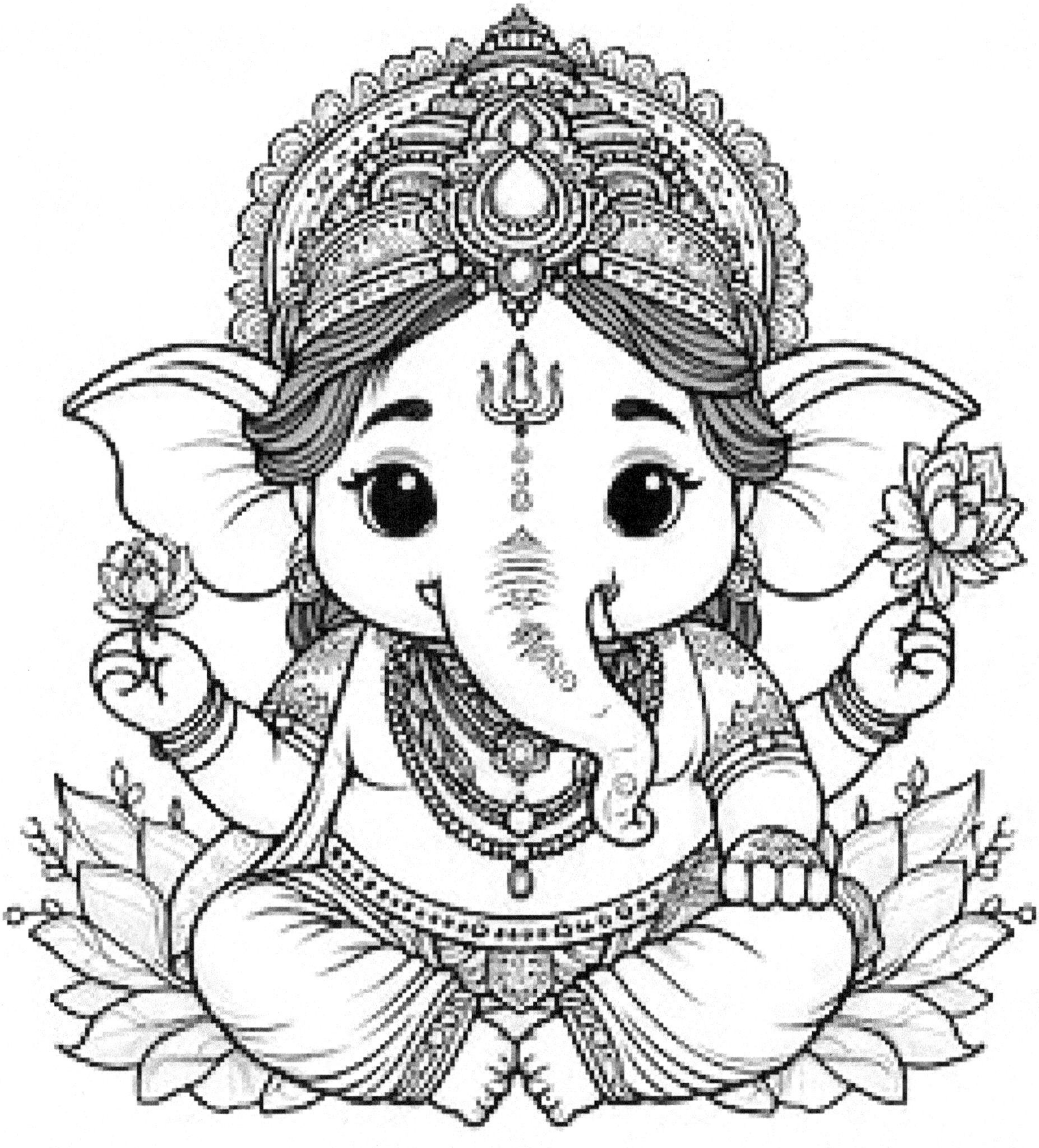

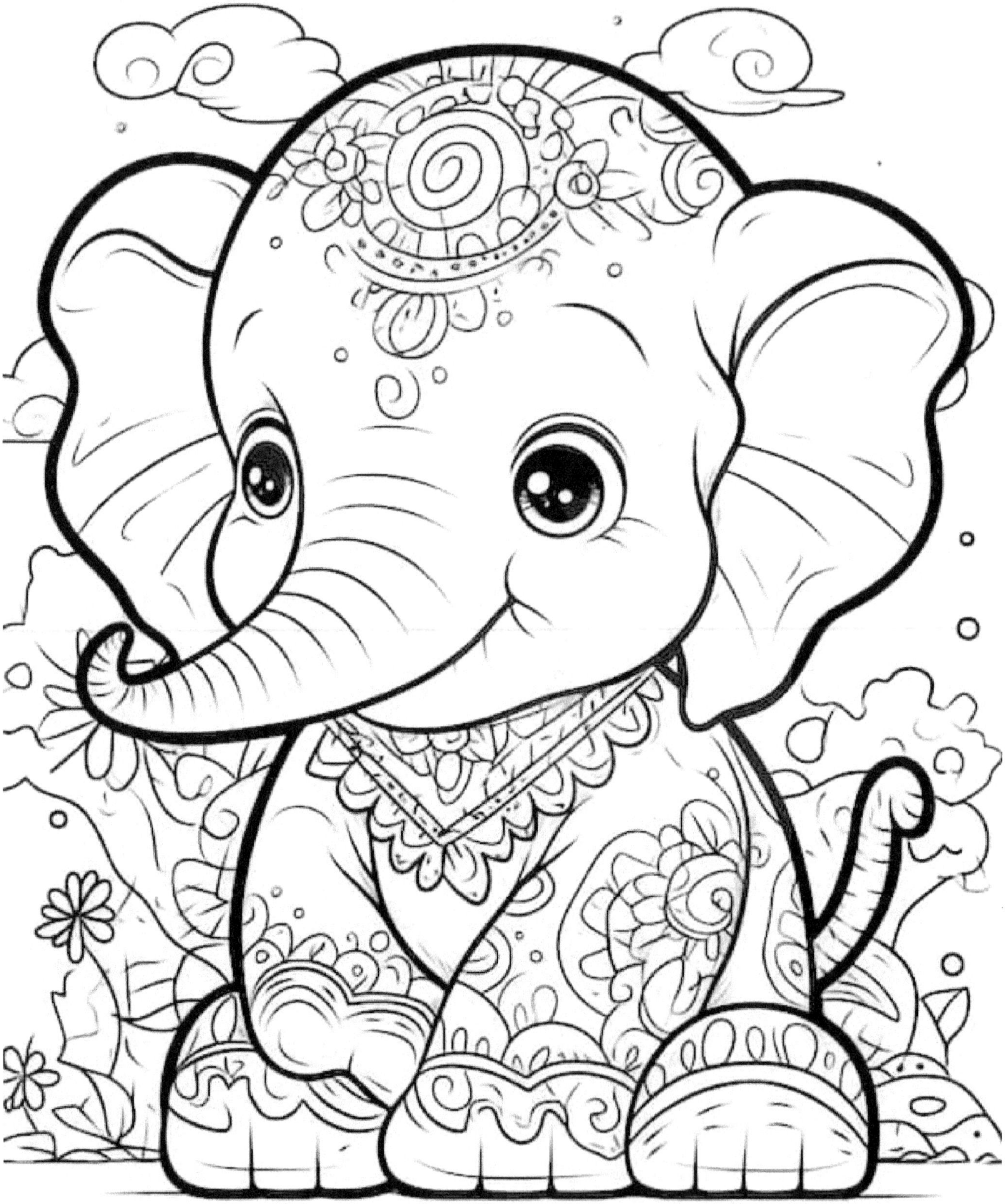

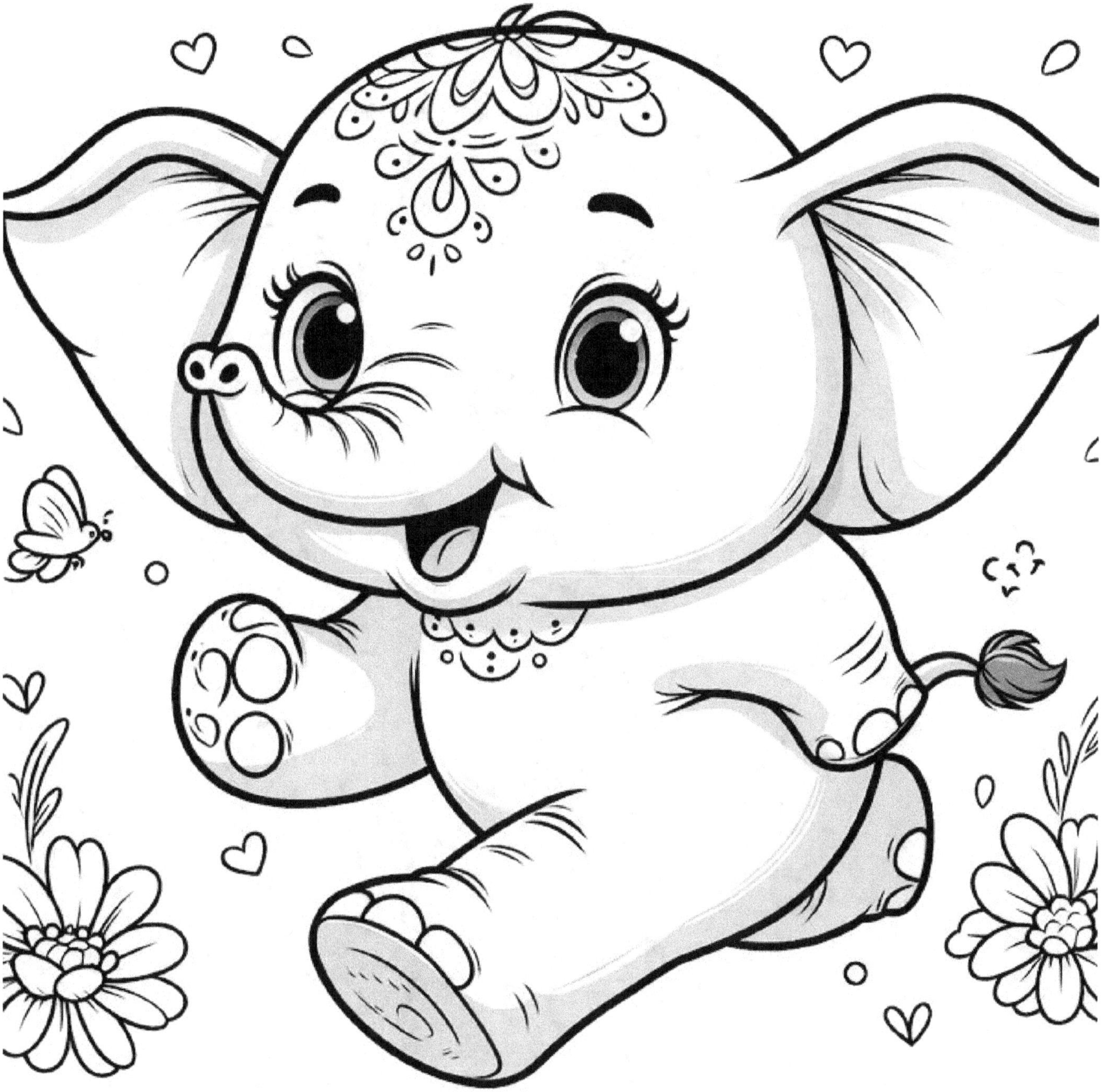

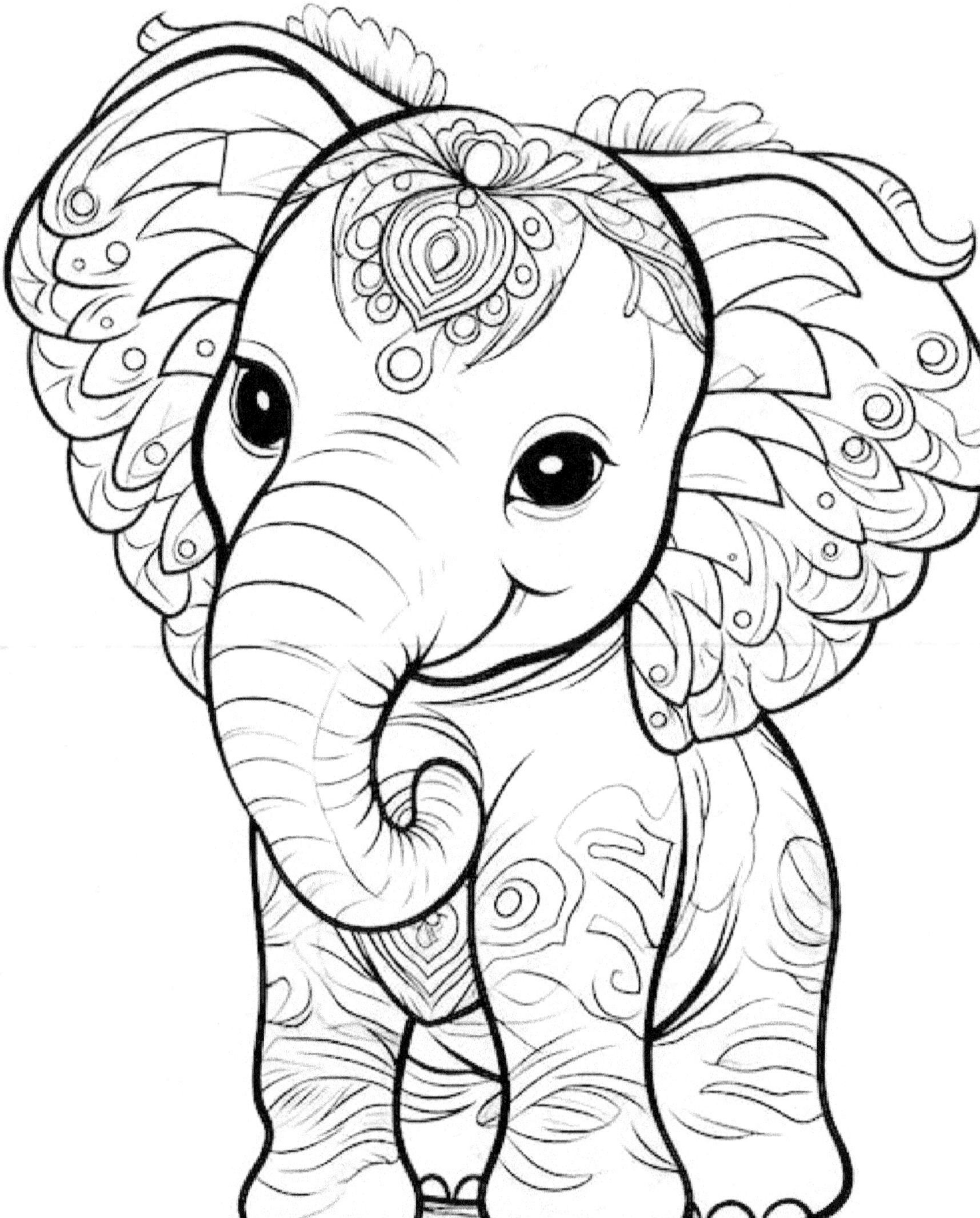

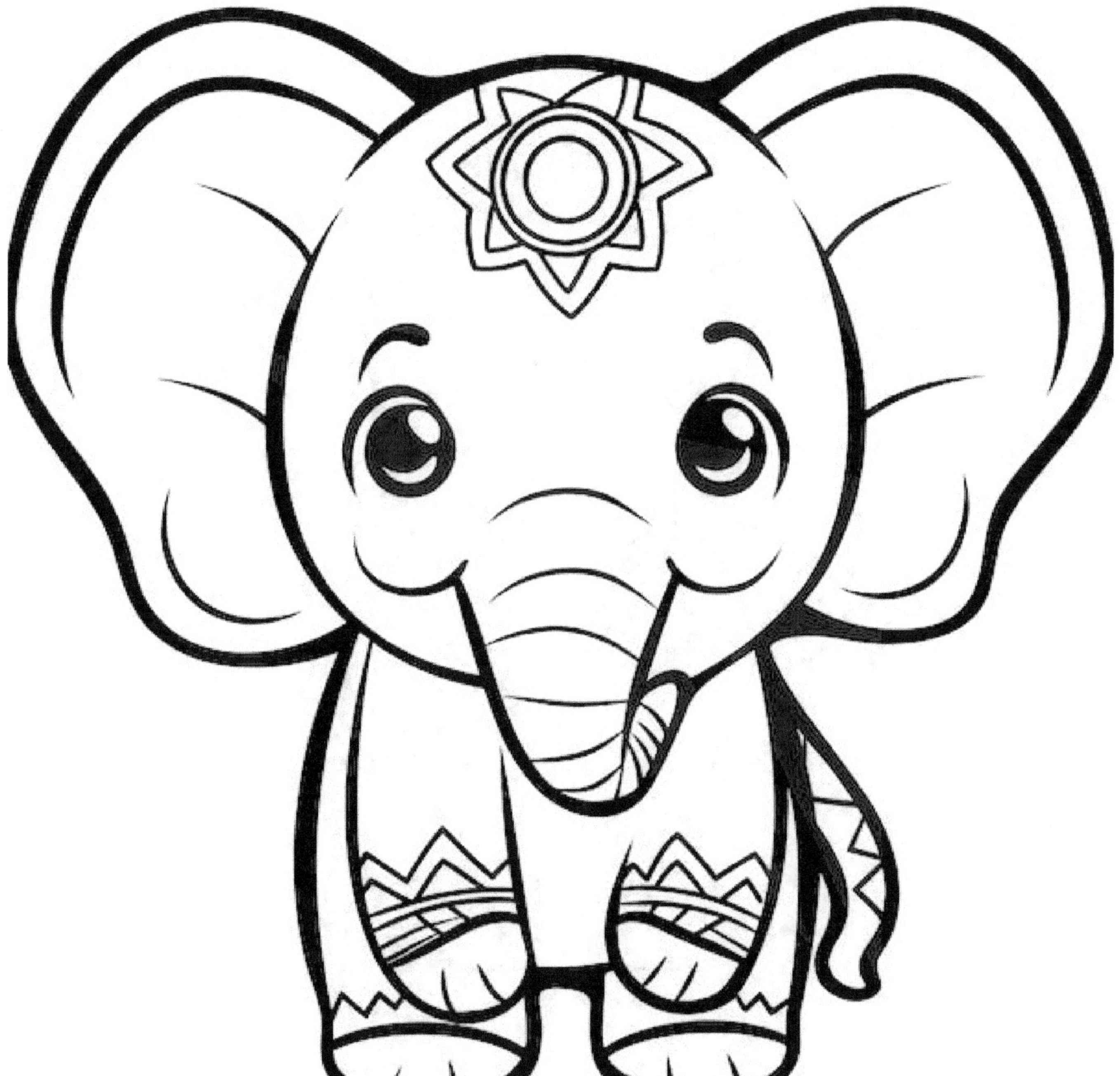

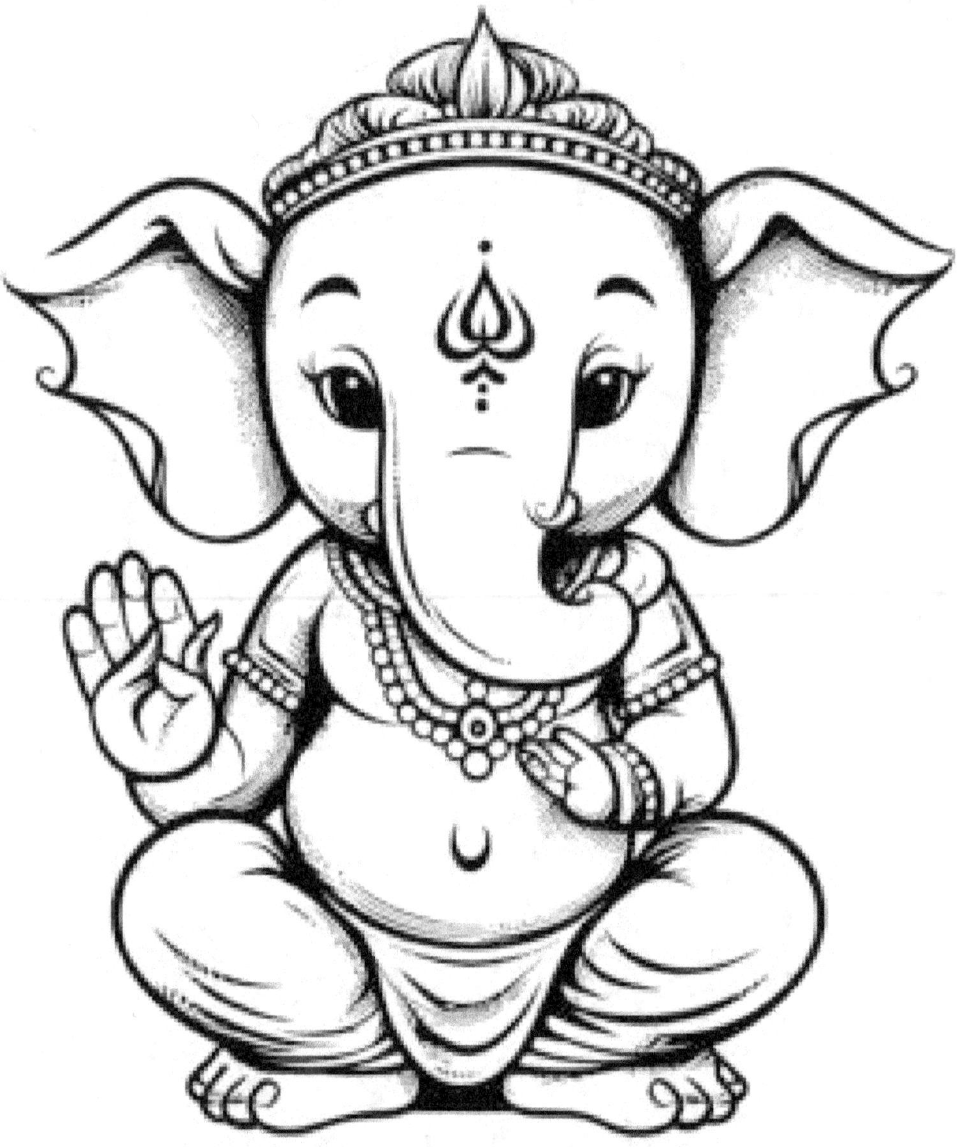

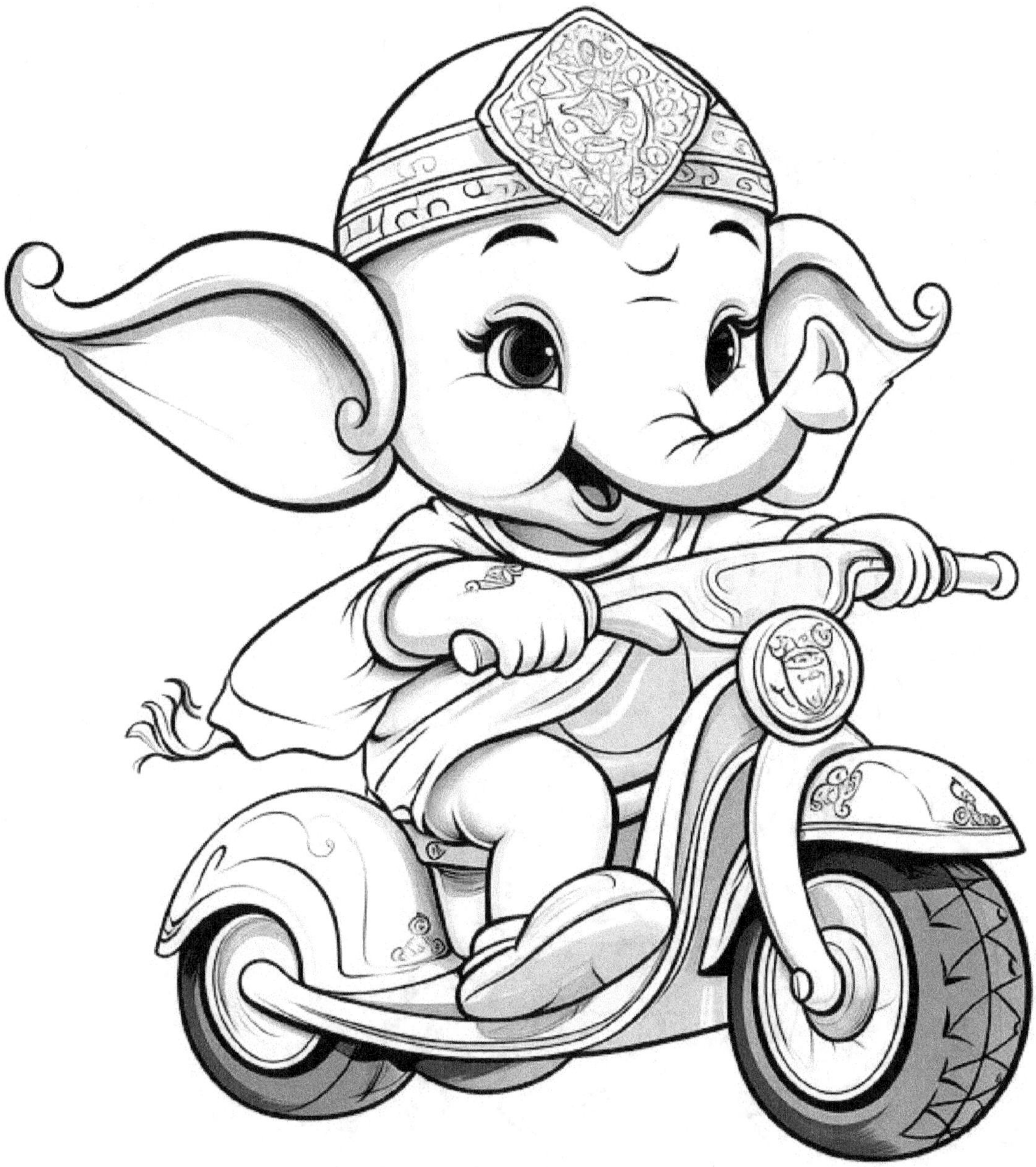

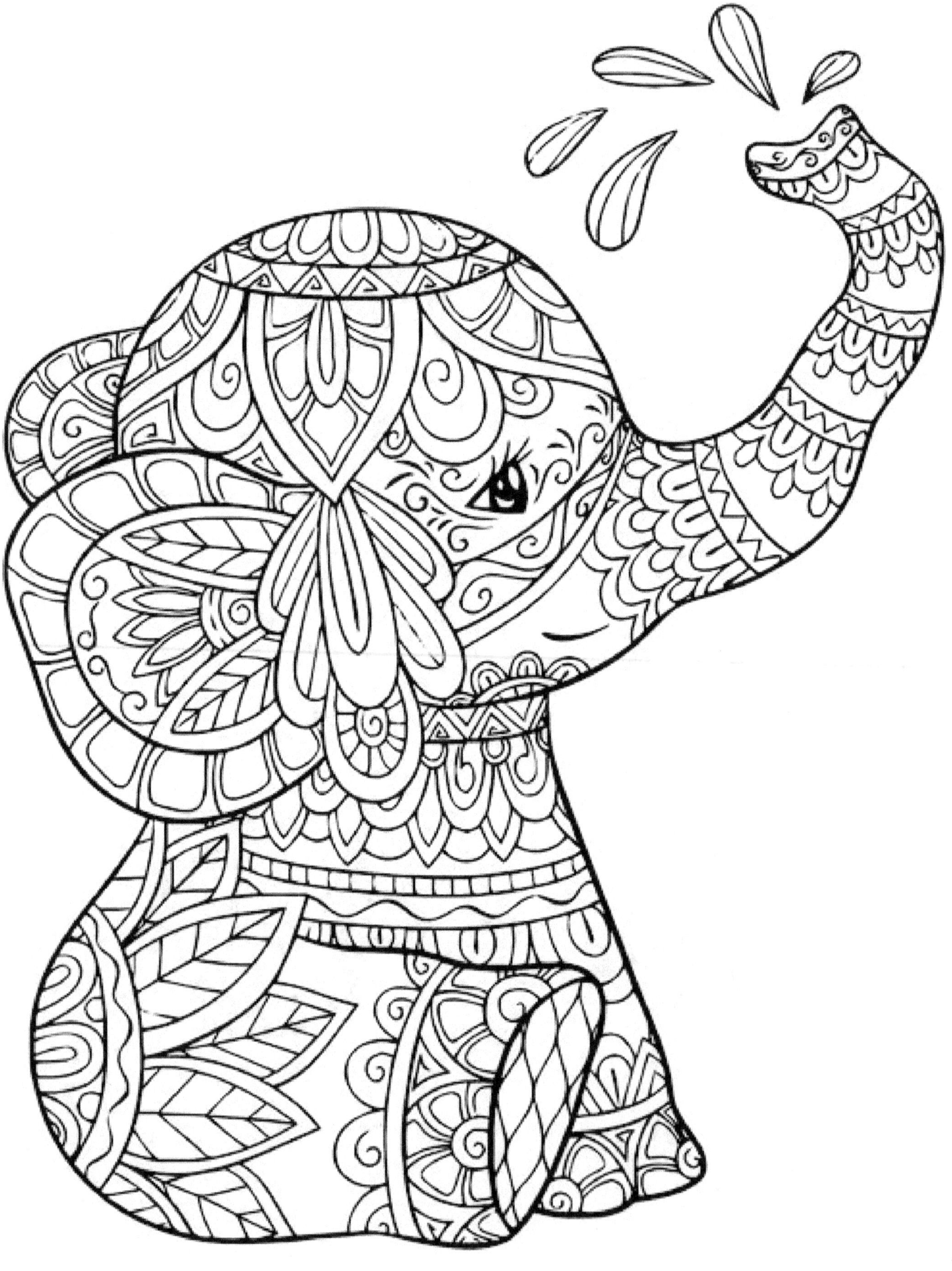

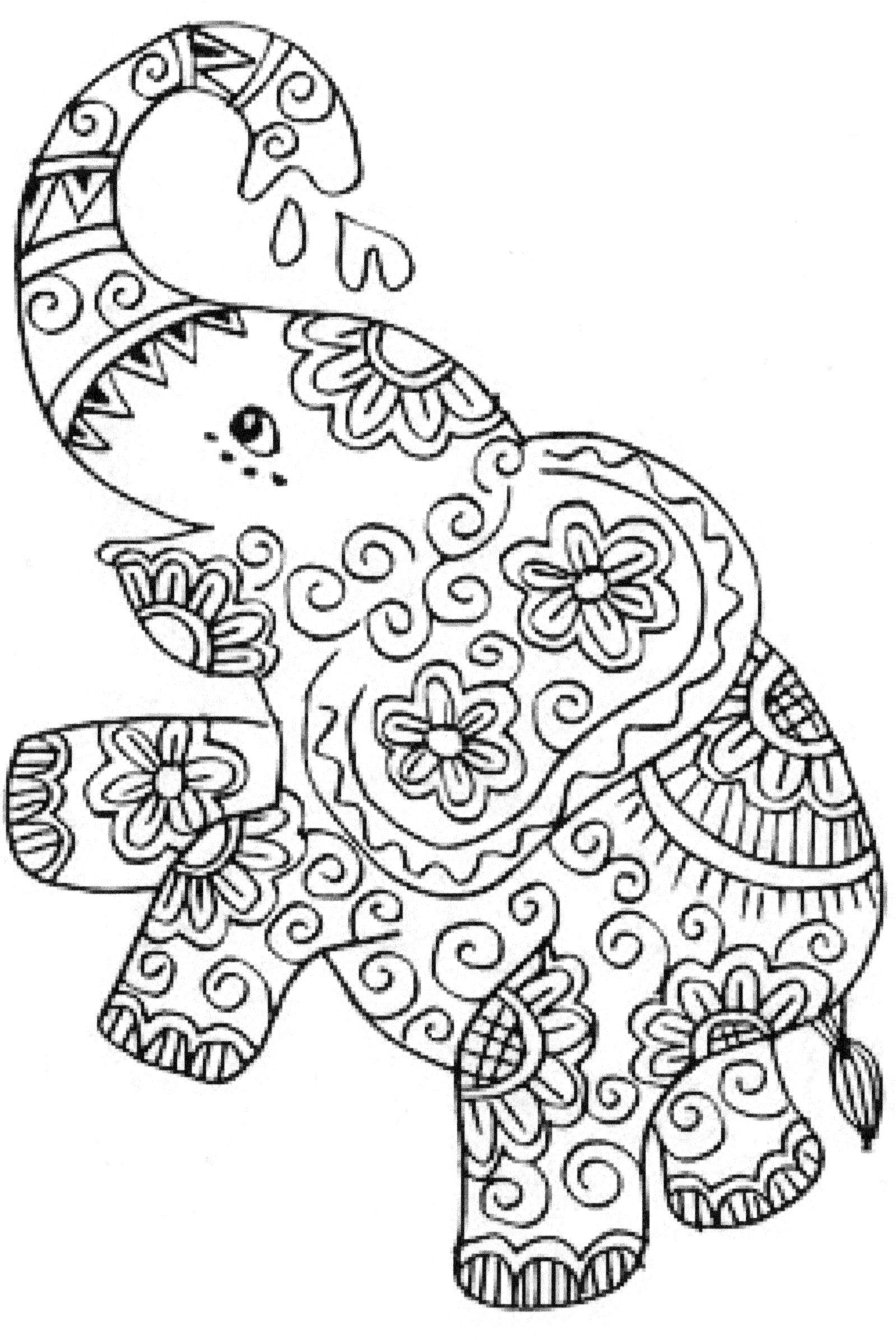

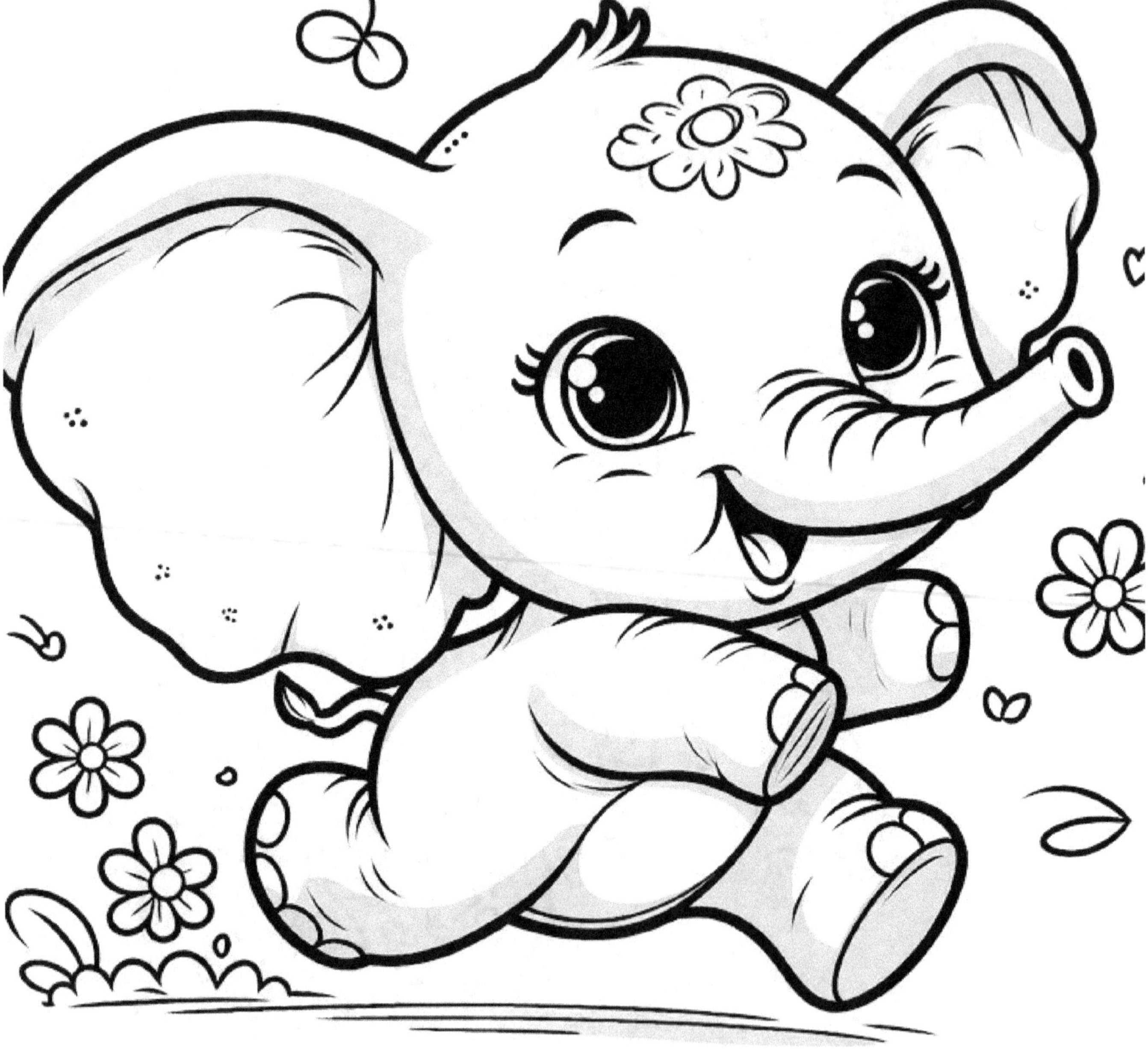

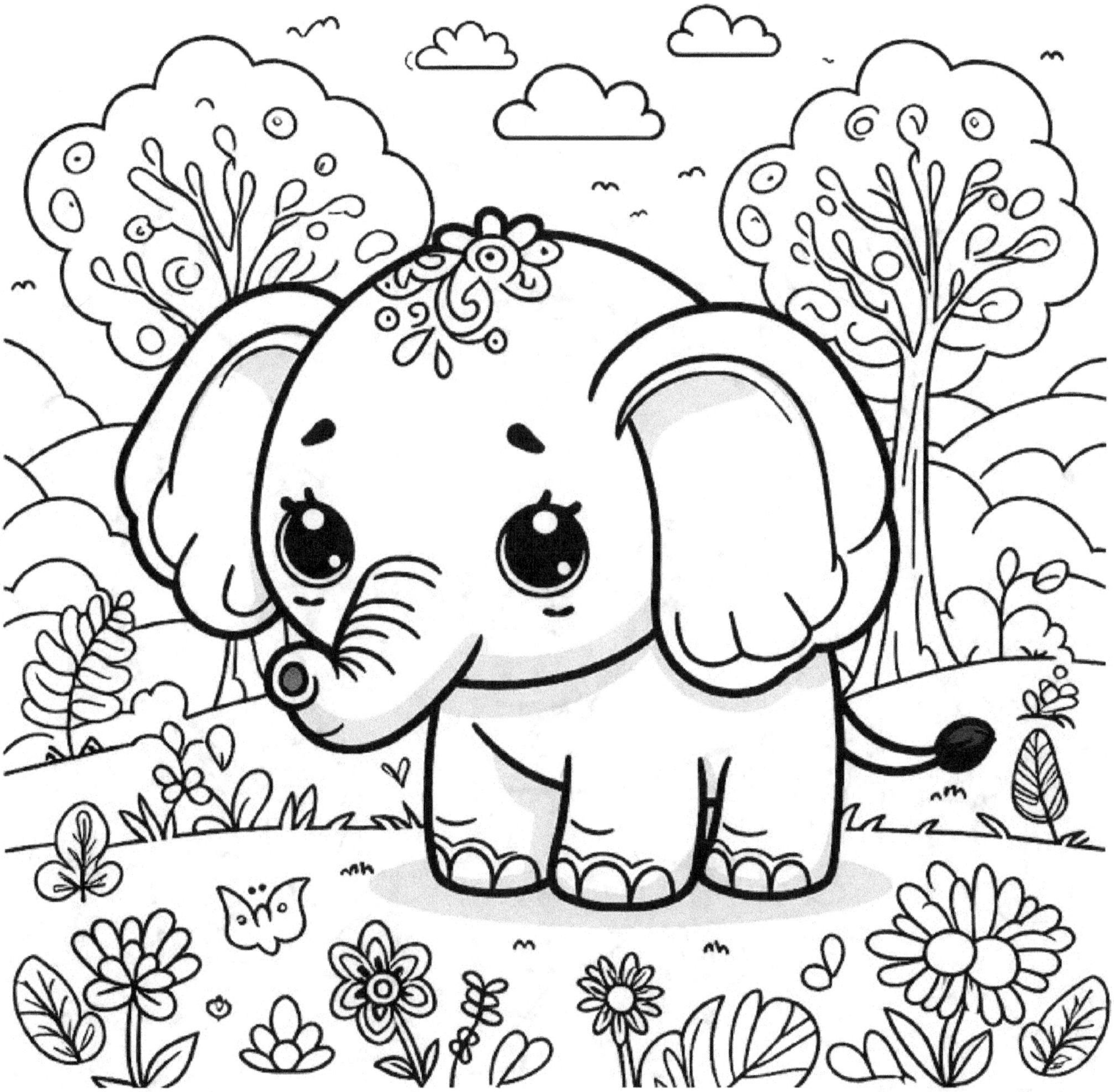

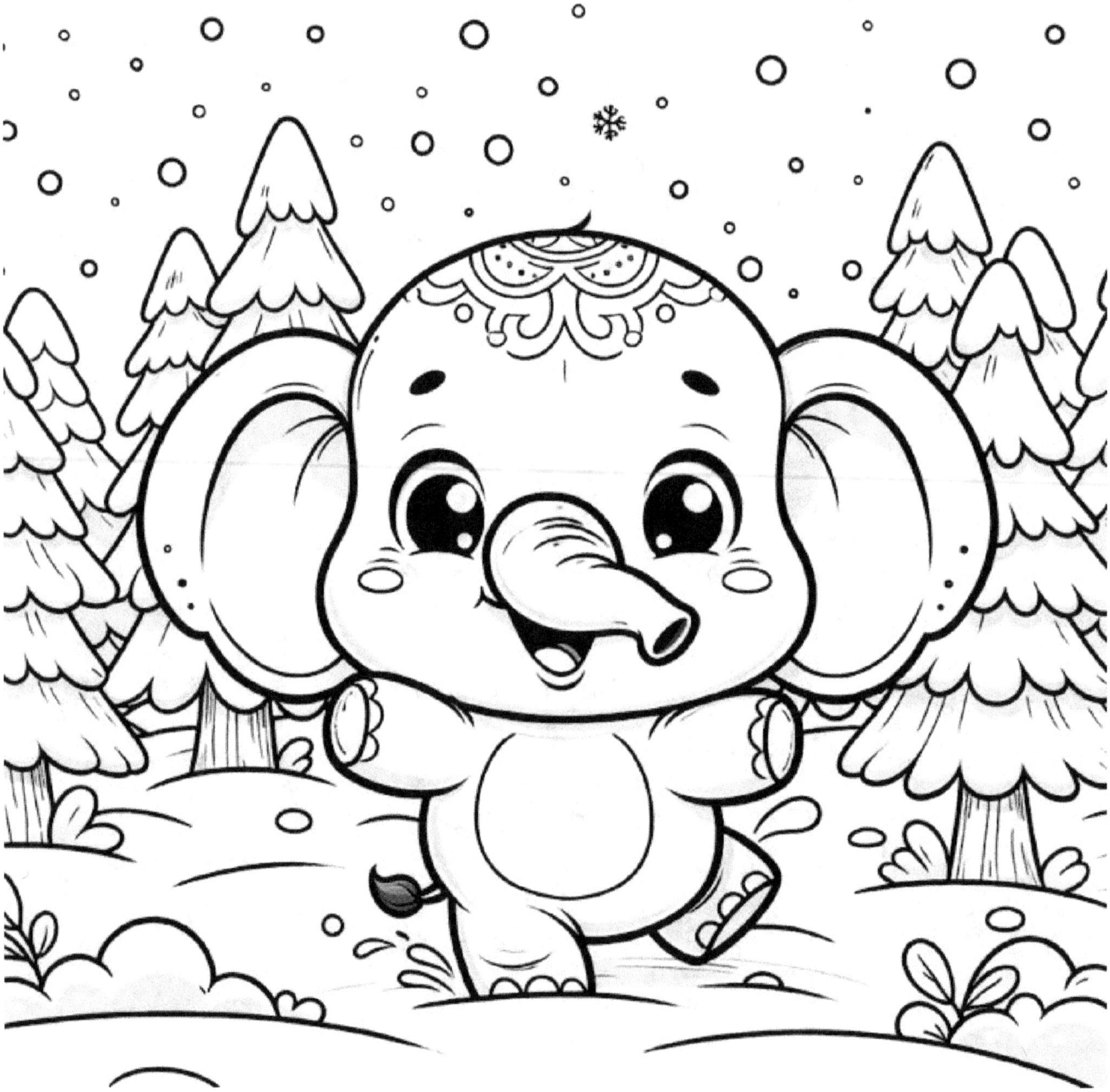

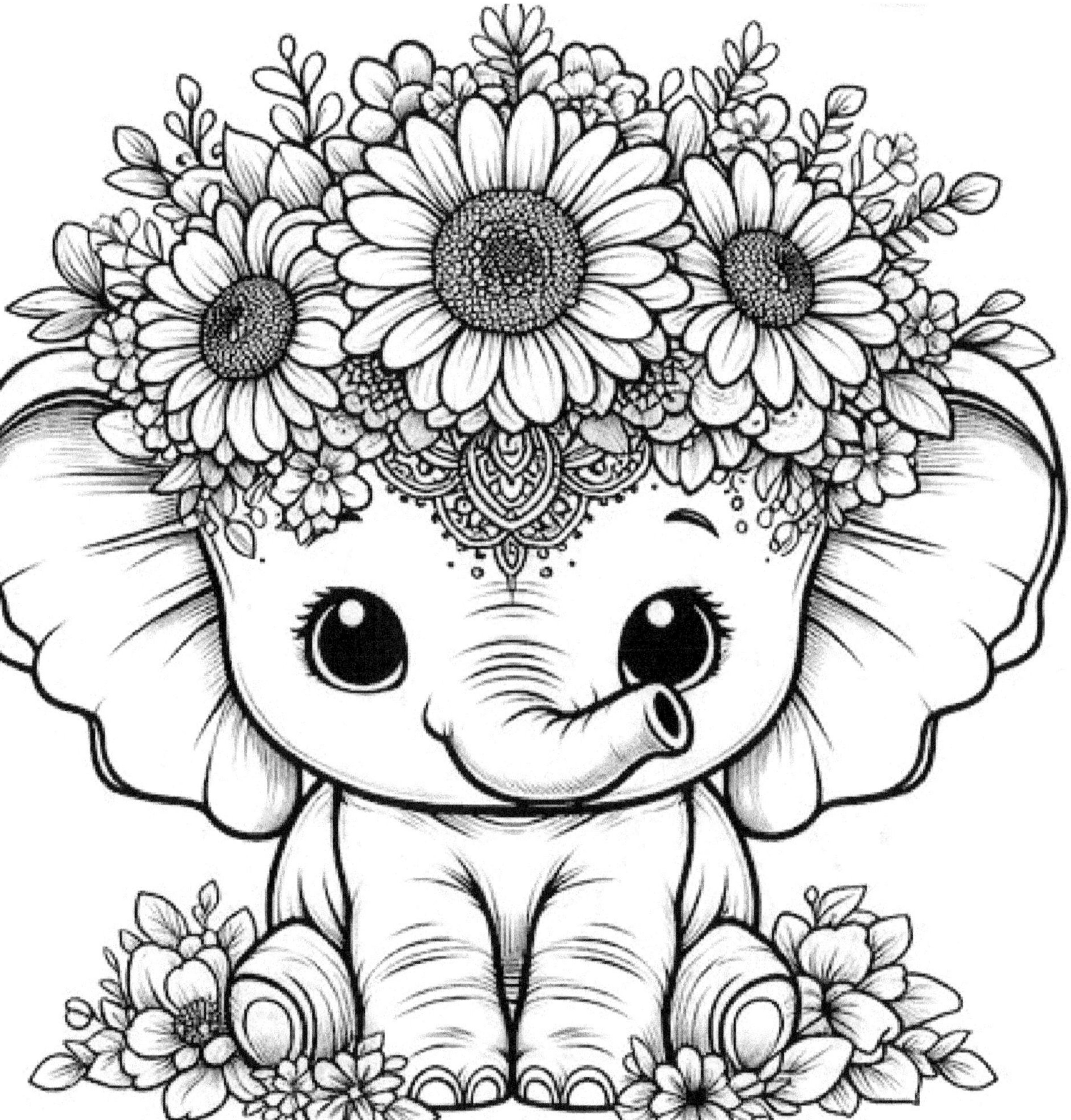

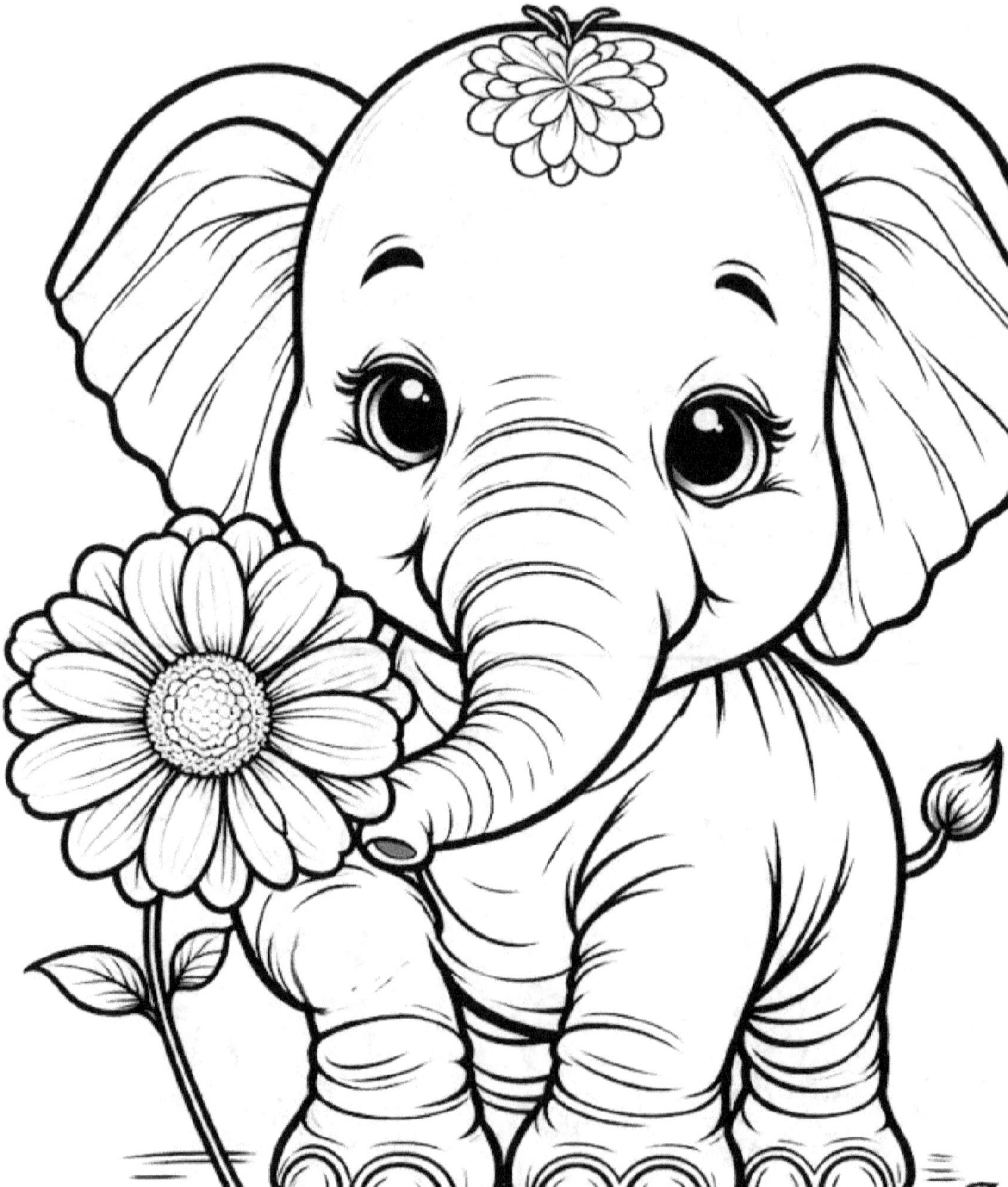

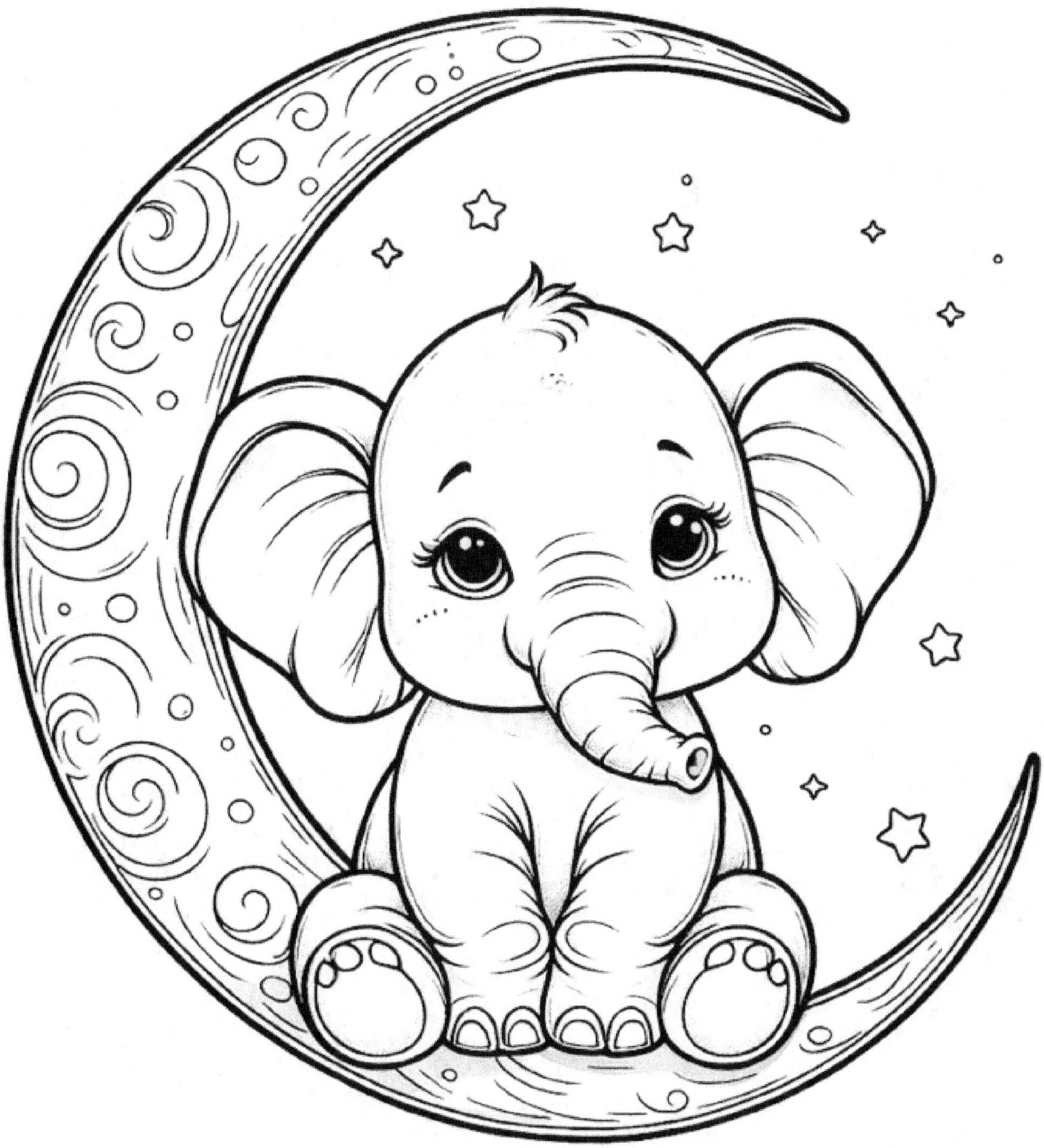

COLORING BOOK

for kids & adults

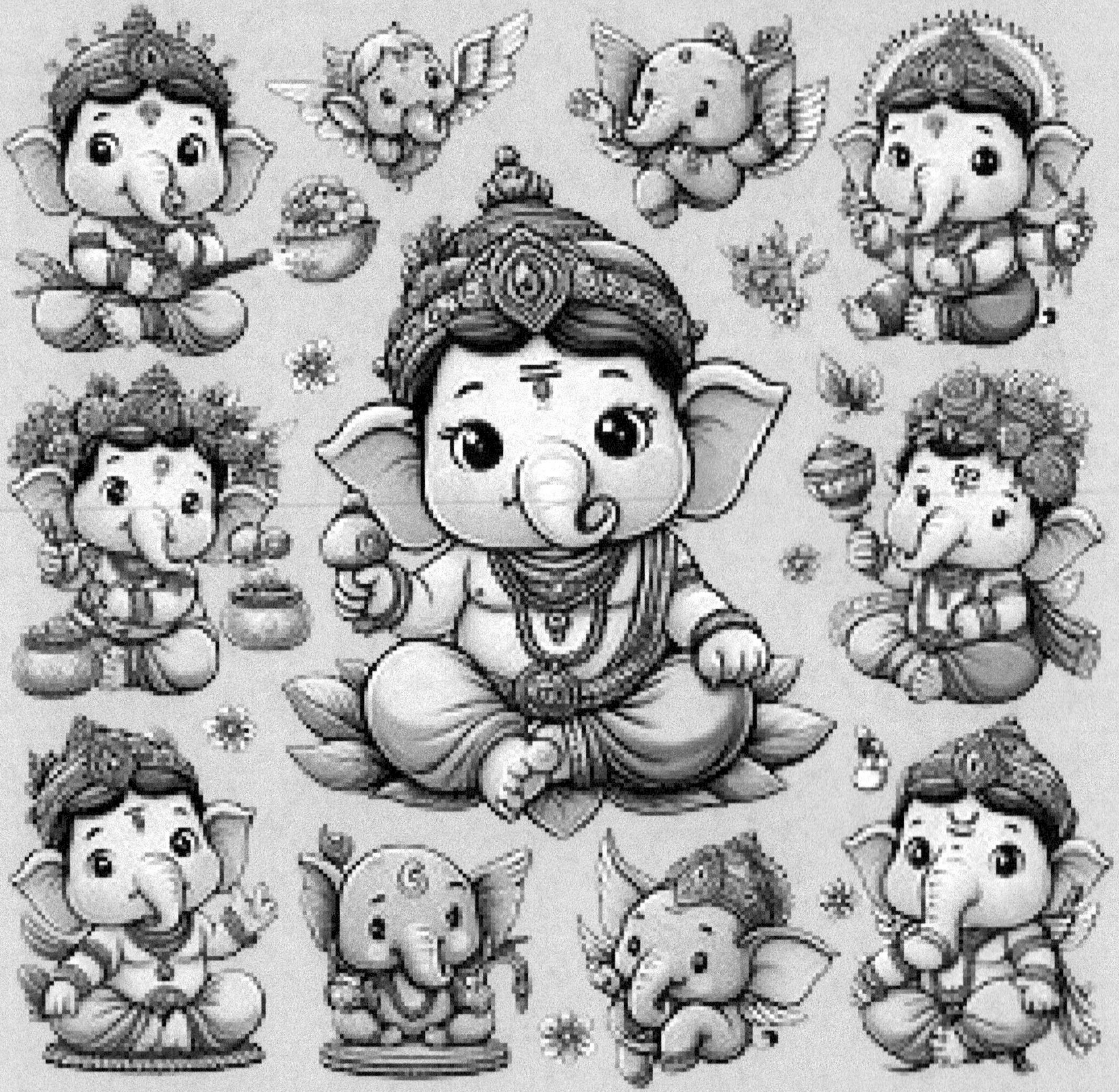

cacho
productos digitales

www.ingramcontent.com/pod-product-compliance
Lightning Source LLC
Chambersburg PA
CBHW062228220526
45471CB00009B/3391
* 9 7 9 8 3 2 3 1 2 5 5 2 4 *